Understanding
The Times

WILLIAM TAYLOR

Understanding The Times

Living in the Light of the Arrival of the King

WILLIAM TAYLOR

ST HELEN'S
MEDIA

CHRISTIAN
FOCUS

Copyright © William Taylor 2009

ISBN 978-1-84550-438-0

10 9 8 7 6 5 4 3 2 1

Published in 2009
by
Christian Focus Publications Ltd.,
Geanies House, Fearn, Tain, Ross-shire,
IV20 1TW, Scotland, UK
www.christianfocus.com
with
St Helen's Media,
Great St Helen's, London
EC3A 6AT, England, UK
www.st-helens.org.uk

Cover design by Moose77.com

Printed and bound by
Norhaven A/S, Denmark

CONTENTS

Preface 7

ONE
The Arrival of the King: Defeating Death 9

TWO
The Arrival of the King: Summoning Sinners .. 29

THREE
The Arrival of the King: Commanding Faith ... 55

FOUR
Understanding the Times of the Kingdom 77

FIVE
Understanding the Terms of the Kingdom 97

SIX
Understanding the Ties of the Kingdom 119

Preface

It is my deep conviction that God works in his mighty power by his Spirit through his Word. Jesus puts it that way in John chapter 6 verse 63: *It is the Spirit who gives life; the flesh is of no avail. The words that I have spoken to you are spirit and life.* It is by Jesus' life-giving and eternal word that his people are born again by the Spirit (1 Pet. 1:23); it is by Jesus' life-giving word that his people grow up to maturity in salvation (1 Pet. 2:2). When Philip asks to be shown the Father (John 14:8), Jesus' answer is framed in terms of the work of the Spirit in giving us his word through the Apostles' teaching. Any mighty work of the Spirit of God and any expression of genuine Christian discipleship will have at its very centre the living word of God. The Bible is the essential bread-and-butter of every Christian's life and growth. Scripture is the vital diet of every healthy church and of every authentic movement of the Spirit.

My desire in writing this book is to help bring the word of God to the people of God through the simple exposition of that word. The aim of Matthew chapters 8–10 within Matthew's gospel is to demonstrate that Jesus has arrived as God's long-promised King. His arrival ushers in a whole new era for humanity and radically affects the future of our world. To live in ignorance of this fact is to fail completely to understand the times in which we live. The aim of this book is to give the reader a clear handle on the days in which we live, so that he or she can order the priorities of life appropriately. In any sphere of life, it is the wise who comprehend the days in which we live and make the required adjustments. In no area is this more pertinent than in relation to Jesus.

The book is essentially a set of edited sermons that were first preached on Sunday mornings at St Helen's and then within the Tuesday lunch-time ministry to business people in the City of London. It is an immense privilege to serve God within a church family that is hungry to be taught God's word, and many of the reflections and discoveries in this book come as a result of conversations and observations made by members of the church family as we have explored the letter together. As with any Bible teaching enterprise, it is very much a 'work in progress'.

I am enormously grateful to Rachel Meek for her painstaking help in editing my transcripts. She has re-written whole sections of the book to make them intelligible! My thanks also to Claire Tunks, my secretary, who has carefully read and re-read each chapter. Without the work of both Claire and Rachel this book would not have come into being.

ONE

The Arrival of the King:
Defeating Death

Matthew 8:1-22

When he came down from the mountain, great crowds followed him. ² And behold, a leper came to him and knelt before him, saying, "Lord, if you will, you can make me clean." ³ And Jesus stretched out his hand and touched him, saying, "I will; be clean." And immediately his leprosy was cleansed. ⁴ And Jesus said to him, "See that you say nothing to anyone, but go, show yourself to the priest and offer the gift that Moses commanded, for a proof to them." ⁵ When he entered Capernaum, a centurion came forward to him, appealing to him, ⁶ "Lord, my servant is lying paralysed at home, suffering terribly." ⁷ And he said to him, "I will come and heal him." ⁸ But the centurion replied, "Lord, I am not worthy to have you come under my roof, but only say the word, and my servant will be healed. ⁹ For I too am a man under authority, with soldiers under me. And I say to one, 'Go,' and he goes, and to another, 'Come,' and he comes, and to my servant, 'Do this,' and he does it." ¹⁰ When Jesus heard this, he marvelled and said to those who followed him, "Truly, I tell you, with no one in Israel have I found such faith. [11] I tell you, many will come from east and west and recline at table with Abraham, Isaac, and Jacob in the kingdom of heaven, [12] while the sons of the kingdom will be thrown into the outer darkness. In that place there will be weeping and gnashing of teeth." [13] And to the centurion Jesus said, "Go; let it be done for you as you have believed." And the servant was healed at that very moment. [14] And when Jesus entered Peter's house, he saw his mother-in-law lying sick with a fever. [15] He touched her hand, and the fever left her, and she rose and began to serve him. [16] That evening they brought to him many who were oppressed by demons, and he cast out the spirits with a word and healed all who were sick. [17] This was to fulfil what was spoken by the prophet Isaiah: "He took our illnesses and bore our diseases." [18] Now when Jesus saw a great crowd around him, he gave orders to go over to the other side. [19] And a scribe came up and said to him, "Teacher, I will follow you wherever you go." [20] And Jesus said to him, "Foxes have holes, and birds of the air have nests, but the Son of Man has nowhere to lay his head." [21] Another of the disciples said to him, "Lord, let me first go and bury my father." [22] And Jesus said to him, "Follow me, and leave the dead to bury their own dead."

On July 7, 2005, Al-Qaeda bombed London. The evening after the bombs went off, I was outside one of the Tube stations involved. I was there in my capacity as a clergyman and I spent the time speaking with emergency workers who had been dealing with the carnage in the tunnels below. Death was nothing new to them. They face it daily.

During a break, I went into one of the churches nearby. In the entrance to the church was the bust of Robert Drew, a famous city merchant of the seventeenth century, who died in 1612. Robert Drew had obviously been something of a big-wig in the city; his bust was dressed in all the finery of a London city dignitary. In those days the great and the good of the City wore wigs and ruffs around their necks! However it wasn't what he was wearing that caught my attention, it was what he was holding. In his hands was a skull. It was impossible to miss the point: all of us will die one day.

Our culture in the West today likes to bury death. That wasn't the case either in the seventeenth century or the centuries surrounding it. The church building where I work was built in the thirteenth century, and all around it are memorials and tombs to people who have died over the last 800 years. Time and again the monuments carry reminders of our human mortality. One has an hour-glass above it, in which the sand has almost finished passing through; its message is clear – 'time is running out'. Many of the monuments include skulls, emphasising the message – 'you too will die one day'. I once saw a monument with a skeleton carved into it, conveying the unmistakable message – 'this is how all mankind will end'.

The Bible depicts death as a sheet, or a shroud, that hangs over all humanity.

> And he will swallow up on this mountain the covering that
> is cast over all peoples, the veil that is spread over all nations
> (Isa. 25:7).

Just as a spread-out sheet completely covers everything below it, so the fact of death is an all-encompassing shroud that envelops mankind. Physical death is an inevitable consequence of our spiritual rebellion against God. This rejection of God's authority, which is what the Bible means by 'sin', demands God's judgment on us all and so, cut off from the author of life, we will surely die.

Matthew chapter 8 presents us with four instances of sickness, death and decay. It is not that any individual's sickness or death is necessarily the direct result of something they did wrong against God. It is rather that Matthew is determined that we should not live with our heads in the sand. He wants some realism about the universal human condition, so he begins this section of his gospel with a stark reminder that death and the certainty of God's judgment awaits every person.

You may feel that this analysis is desperately bleak, and you may object to such a starkly negative opening to this book. However, Matthew's aim in this part of his gospel is that we should come to understand the days in which we live. It is only as we open our eyes to analyse honestly the true condition of our world that we shall be able to make sense of the world and of what Jesus came to do in it. By contrast, our culture would have us play the ostrich and bury the reality of death and God's judgment, with the result that our culture sees little value either in Jesus or in his work. We would much rather not talk about death, or at most we would prefer only to mention death hand-in-hand with the kind of sentimental platitudes that we hear in songs like 'The Circle of Life' in Walt Disney's *The Lion King*, which speaks of *'great and small on the endless round... on the path unwinding in the circle of life'*. Matthew wants his readers to be realists who face up to the facts and certainties of this world, rather than sentimentalists who turn a blind eye to them. It is only as we come to terms with death and God's judgment that we shall begin to grasp just how significant and universally vital Jesus and his work are.

Sin, God's judgment and the shadow of death

In the first scene of chapter 8 (verses 1-4), we meet a leper. In Jesus' day, leprosy was a catch-all medical term for a number of skin conditions, some more serious than others. However, those with more developed forms of the disease were considered to be as good as dead already. The medics tell us that as a patient's condition deteriorates, the skin becomes scaly and white, and the sufferer takes on the appearance of a dying man. In the first century, leprosy was feared as much as cancer, AIDS or Avian flu is today. A man with leprosy had the appearance of death; he carried the stench of death; and he was quite clearly under the sentence of death. Leprosy was no 'man flu'.

The seriousness with which leprosy was regarded is illustrated by two Old Testament examples. When Moses' sister Miriam was struck down with leprosy, Aaron said, 'Let her not be as one dead, whose flesh is half-eaten away' (Numbers 12 verse 12). When Naaman sought healing from King Jehoram, Jehoram complained, 'Am I God to kill and make alive?' (2 Kings 5 verse 7). Clearly, in both cases, to have leprosy was regarded as a death sentence.

However, Matthew has more than simply physical death in mind when relating this story. Since the leper was as good as dead, he would have been seen in Israel as a living embodiment of God's judgment, for physical death in the Bible is a consequence of spiritual death. We die because we are cut off from God, the author of life, and physical death in the Bible is a sure sign of judgment to follow.

> Just as it is appointed for man to die once and after that comes judgment (Heb. 9:27).

As a result, it is not surprising that lepers were regarded as unclean. They were excluded from the people of God, they were shut out from his presence in the temple, and should a leper be healed, he had to make a sacrifice of atonement for his spiritual cleansing if he was to be readmitted amongst God's people[1].

This view of leprosy and other sickness and disease ties in with the promise of blessings and curses made to God's people in the Old Testament (see Deuteronomy 28 and 2 Chronicles 6). Positively, the land of Israel was intended to be like Eden, a place of blessing and bounty, so that as the people of Israel lived perfectly

---

[1] Leviticus 14:2 – 32

under God's rule in the land they would be a beacon, holding out the offer of life and light to the nations around them. Negatively, if they rejected God, they would become like any other nation – subject to God's judgment and condemnation. These judgments included the skin diseases known as 'leprosy', which were a living symbol of spiritual and physical death.

So then, the presence of this leper in God's promised land was a painful picture of God's nation and world out of relationship with the life-giving creator. Each and every human being across the globe has engaged in his or her own personal rebellion against God and so each and every human being is touched by sin and God's judgment and is covered by the shroud of death. (See Preacher's Note 1 at the end of the chapter)

We have no idea in this case whether leprosy was a direct result of the leper's particular sin or not. Sometimes in the Bible sickness clearly is the result of specific sins; more frequently it is not. Whatever the case in this instance, all people had to do was catch a glimpse of him, or hear the rattle of his warning bell, or a snatch of his cry, 'Unclean!' and they were reminded of the universal condition of humanity, just as I was at the tomb of Robert Drew.

Although this study concentrates on the story of the leper, the same theme runs right the way through the next three scenes from verse 5 to verse 17. Each one is a picture of the sickness, suffering and death that flows from living in a fallen world under God's judgment. Once again, it must be stressed that it is not necessarily any individual, personal sin that is the cause of sickness. The centurion's servant was paralysed and 'suffering terribly'; a painful, lingering death was the most likely outcome. Peter's mother-in-law had a fever[2] which, without penicillin, was

---

[2] Peter G Bolt has demonstrated the close association between fever and death in the ancient world in his book *Jesus' Defeat of Death: Persuading Mark's Early Readers*, Society for New Testament Studies Monograph Series 125, Cambridge University Press, 2003. He lists

life-threatening in the first century. These two scenes, together with the sick and demon-possessed of Capernaum, present a grim picture of God's land and serve as a reminder of the death, the decay and the inevitability of God's judgment that we all face.

In so-called sophisticated London, at the heart of one of the world's most vibrant financial sectors, where people are so clued up about so many things, we are desperately naïve when it comes to death. We have health plans and pension plans and holiday plans, but my experience is that people rarely pause to consider the reality of our human condition. As I think of just one small community with which I am familiar, it occurs to me that, without exception, every family is touched by some form of physical, emotional or psychological suffering. One has a life-long debilitating illness to cope with, another a child facing decades of disability; others have to cope with serious mental illness or deep and desperate depression, whilst others have the problems and burdens of approaching old age – weakness, dementia and increasing dependency. All of us are touched by the reality of an imperfect world. All of us face disease, decay and death. In one three-month period recently I was involved in the funerals of three City business people. One was aged 53, another 43 and the third was only 30. (Preacher's Note 2)

When I'm speaking on a Sunday at St Helen's or at the lunchtime City services, I sometimes suggest that we would be wise to make a computer screen-saver with a picture of ourselves in a coffin – just to remind us of our ultimate destiny. We are told that people on death row notch off the days to their death, but there is in reality little difference between those who know

---

various sources such as Epictetus: "What do the swords of tyrants do? They kill. And what does fever do? Nothing else." (p. 80), and Philo: "Fever... generally reaches the crisis on the seventh day; for this day decides the struggle for life, bringing to some recovery, to others death." (p. 82).

the total and we who don't. Our days are still numbered. After death, we will face God and his judgment, for we too have lived with God our creator pushed to the fringes of our lives. To use the spiritual imagery of the leper, we too are unclean, we too live in a world under judgment, and outside of Jesus Christ we are spiritually dead. It is the universal condition of humanity from London to Lima, from Sydney to Siberia and from the Arctic to the Antarctic.

Matthew chapter 8 verses 1-22 introduces us to sin, God's judgment and the shadow of death. However, whilst Matthew wants us to come face to face with these facts of life, he also wants to introduce us to the solution in these verses.

Jesus, God's King, and the reversal of death

The aim of this section of Matthew's gospel is to show us that Jesus has arrived as God's King and Saviour and that he has come with all of God's authority to satisfy God's judgment and to reverse the reality of death and judgment for his people. This means that now, as then, we live in a day when God's solution for death and judgment, for sin and condemnation, is open and available to all who will submit to the divine authority of God's chosen King, Jesus Christ.

Matthew's gospel can be divided into 5 major sections (Preacher's Note 3). Each section is made up of a 'narrative' followed by a 'discourse'. In each case the narrative describes the actions of Jesus, whilst the discourse contains teaching which explains those actions. The section studied in this book is the second one, running from chapter 8 through to chapter 10, which might be titled *The Arrival of the King*. Chapters 8 and 9 contain the narrative, and chapter 10 the teaching-discourse with Jesus' disciples. Matthew's third section begins in chapter 11 with a summary of this key lesson of section two, as John the Baptist sends his disciples to ask Jesus the burning question: *are you the one who is to come, or shall we look for another?* (11 verse 3) Jesus answers

John's disciples: *go and tell John what you hear and see*. Jesus then runs through everything that has happened in the narrative section of chapters 8 and 9:

> the blind receive their sight and the lame walk, lepers are cleansed and the deaf hear, and the dead are raised up, and the poor have good news preached to them. And blessed is the one who is not offended by me.

In other words, yes, I am the one who is to come. I have arrived. The King is here with all of God's authority to provide God's solution to the universal condition of humanity. The point had been clearly demonstrated by Jesus' healing of the leper, Peter's mother-in-law and the demon-possessed and sick of Capernaum, and through his dealings with the centurion. *The Arrival of the King* certainly seems an appropriate title for this section of Matthew's Gospel.

As chapter 8 opens, Jesus is surrounded by people. However, even as the 'vast crowds' swarm around him, Matthew wants to focus our attention on one individual.

> Behold, a leper came to him and knelt before him saying, "Lord, if you will, you can make me clean."

This leper would have known no human contact for years. He would have lived life shut off from his loved ones. He would not have hugged his wife or played with his children. He may have caught a glimpse of them as they drew near from a distance and left a token of their affection, but then they would have backed off. As the leper approached Jesus, we can imagine the crowd stepping aside, mothers pulling back their children, on-lookers covering their mouths and noses for fear of contamination. Then the leper literally threw himself on the ground before Jesus, and uttered his desperate plea:

> "Lord, if you will, you can make me clean."

Matthew says that the man '*knelt before*' Jesus, and the word translated in this way is the same as the word used for the Magi in chapter 2 verses 2 and 11, where it is translated '*they worshipped him*'. The leper was recognising the divine authority of Jesus even as he made this amazing statement. Notice that he said not, 'If you *can*' but 'if you *will*'.

The split-second pause between verse 2 and verse 3 of chapter 8 must have appeared as an eternity to this poor man. But it was not only the leper whose future was dependent upon Jesus' answer. As we wait for Jesus' reply, it's as if eternity hangs in the balance for the whole human race as well. For if Jesus *will* reach out and touch this unclean man under the shadow of death, then there is hope for humanity enveloped, as we are, by the shroud of death; if not, then Jesus has no solution to the human condition. How does Matthew continue his account?

> And Jesus stretched out his hand and touched him, saying, "I will; be clean". And immediately his leprosy was cleansed.

We are introduced to Jesus. He is God's long-awaited King; he has come with all God's power and authority to deal with sin, death and God's judgment; he has the power to reverse the sentence of death.

Jesus' encounter with the Roman centurion in verses 5-13 takes things one stage further. When God promised the arrival of his great rescuing King in the Old Testament, the day of his coming was explained using the language of a great and glorious banquet. Perhaps one of the clearest passages that spells out the promise is contained in Isaiah 25 verses 6-9:

> On this mountain the LORD of hosts will make for all peoples a feast of rich food, a feast of well-aged wine, of rich food full of marrow, of aged wine well refined. And he will swallow up on this mountain the covering that is cast over all peoples, the veil that is spread over all nations. He will swallow up death forever; and the Lord GOD will wipe away

tears from all faces, and the reproach of his people he will take away from all the earth, for the LORD has spoken. It will be said on that day, "Behold, this is our God; we have waited for him, that he might save us. This is the LORD; we have waited for him; let us be glad and rejoice in his salvation."

The food on the menu at this banquet seems to be a combination of Jamie Oliver and Marco Pierre White! The wine is the finest vintage from the vineyards of Bordeaux. The benefits of this banquet include the removal of '*the covering that is cast over all peoples, the veil that is spread over all nations, he will swallow up death forever. And the Lord will wipe away tears from all faces and the reproaches of his people he will take away from the earth.*' The people of Israel were waiting for God's long-promised Messiah, who was going to come with all of God's divine authority to overthrow the effects of human sinfulness (including God's condemnation, judgment and death) and institute this glorious banquet. It is particularly significant that those who benefit from this banquet include those from '*all peoples*' and '*all nations*'.

This background knowledge makes Jesus' words and their effect of immense universal and eternal significance. The centurion recognised the sovereign authority of Jesus. He saw that Jesus had all of God's power to overthrow and reverse the universal condition of humanity. This centurion was a foreigner to Israel and yet in response to his trust in Jesus, Jesus promised him that '*many will come from east and west and recline at table with Abraham, and Isaac, and Jacob in the kingdom of heaven*'. Jesus had come not just for the Jews, but for people from every nation. The announcement of the arrival of God's kingdom on earth was as relevant for the Roman centurion as for the Jewish leper.

The healing of Peter's mother-in-law, in verses 14-15, makes it clear that Jesus' conquering authority extends to women too, a revolutionary message in a society which regarded women as property, and where a woman's word counted for little in legal terms. It is significant that Matthew tells us that '*Jesus touched her hand*'. Just as he had publicly demonstrated the leper's restoration to society by touching him, Jesus showed that this woman was a precious member of his people. As Jesus went on to heal people possessed by demons and with diseases which made them ritually unclean (verse 16), the same point is made, and the message is reinforced that Jesus has come as God's long-awaited King with divine authority to give hope of rescue to every manner and condition of humanity.

I recently flew from London to Sydney. The route is fairly direct out of Heathrow, heading south across the Channel and down across Europe. As we flew, it was possible to follow our progress on a monitor on the seat in front of me. As we flew over Europe, I was reminded of the truth of this study, namely that below us were literally tens of millions facing the universal condition of humanity – sin and God's judgment. As we made our way across the top of India and Pakistan and over the Bay of Bengal, I could not help thinking again of the millions more men and women – each one destined to die and to face God in judgment. We continued around the edge of the South China Sea into Indonesia, aware of innumerable others in the same predicament. But Jesus Christ has arrived as God's King with the solution to the universal human condition. He has absolute authority over each and every one of them. Christ alone holds the key to the reversal of death and the solution to each one's greatest need.

It is possible sometimes to forget the sheer scale and the scope of the gospel claims. No one is excluded from the universal condition of humanity. Everyone is included in God's offer of hope and of salvation. The gospel is for the centurion, for the leper, for Peter's mother-in-law and for the '*many who will come from east and west and recline at table with Abraham, Isaac and Jacob*'. Jesus has arrived. He has all of God's absolute power to provide the solution to the universal condition of all mankind.

The cross, Jesus' death and his payment for sin

This brings us to the final point, as we ask ourselves: 'How then can Jesus do this?'

Matthew gives us the answer in at least two places. In verse 4, Jesus said to the leper:

> "See that you say nothing to anyone, but go, show yourself to the priest and offer the gift that Moses commanded for a proof to them."

It may be that Jesus sent the leper to the priest simply to fulfil the requirements of the law, for if a person did recover from leprosy, he had to go to the priest to show that he had been cleansed (Leviticus 14). Once he had made his sacrifice for atonement, then he could be accepted back amongst God's people. If that is the sense of the verse, then the word 'proof' would mean that the leper was to show himself to the priest and to offer his sacrifice as evidence that he was now better. However, the word 'proof' could just as easily relate to Jesus, his identity and work, as to the leper and his healing. If that is the case, then the leper's appearance in the temple, healed, would have functioned as a proof to the priest of the identity of Jesus as the long-awaited one who had come with all God's authority to deal with the problem of sin, death and judgment.

This reading of the verse makes all the more sense when we consider where Matthew 8 verses 1-4 comes in the overall context of the gospel. The leper's healing comes immediately after the Sermon on the Mount, in which Jesus had been announcing his kingdom standards. Part of his announcement of the kingdom was a spelling out of the law and of the requirements of the law. In his restatement of the law, Jesus showed how absolute are God's demands for perfect living if a person is to be fit for God's kingdom. It is impossible to come away from the Sermon on the Mount without a deep sense of one's own personal failure and spiritual inadequacy, as God's law condemns. Starting with the beatitude '*blessed are the poor in spirit*', Jesus went on to say:

"I tell you, unless your righteousness exceeds that of the scribes and Pharisees, you will never enter the kingdom of heaven." (Matthew 5 verse 20);

"You therefore must be perfect, as your heavenly Father is perfect." (verse 48)

"You have heard that it was said to those of old, 'You shall not murder; and whoever murders will be liable to judgment.' But I say to you that everyone who is angry with his brother will be liable to judgment." (verses 21-22)

I can remember only too well being taught the Sermon on the Mount over an eight-week series as a young Christian back in the 1980s. For those eight weeks we almost crawled from our pews as we heard the perfect requirements of Jesus for those who would live in his kingdom. Yet as we come to the end of the Sermon and start this new section of the Gospel in Matthew chapter 8, what is the first thing we are confronted with? A leper! Here is a man who is a powerful and clear symbol of rebellious Israel still in exile under the shroud of sin, death and God's judgment. As the leper turned up in the temple, his healed existence announced to the priests that they were redundant, that the long-promised King had arrived, with all God's power and authority to reverse the effects of the Fall by satisfying God's judgment on sin. It was the law of God that pronounced the sentence of spiritual death and separation on the leper. But by telling this man to show himself to the priest at the temple (verse 4), Jesus at least hinted at his intention to fulfil the atoning sacrifices of the Old Testament and provide God's long-awaited solution to the wretched condition of our fallen world which stands condemned under God's law.[3]

However, if we are not convinced by this reading of verse 4,

---

[3] We shall see more about this in chapter 3 as we come to the end of the narrative section of these chapters.

that Jesus' authority and power are being vindicated, then by the time we get to verse 17 we find Matthew concluding this group of healing stories with a quotation from Isaiah 53 verse 4. This chapter of Isaiah is one of the most significant of those passages in the Old Testament which look forward to the cross. By quoting from it in chapter 8:17, Matthew is saying to us that this is how Jesus is going to achieve what he promised – to reverse the effects of this fallen world. God's King has arrived with all of God's authority over death, disease and decay, but he is not only the King, he is also the suffering servant of Isaiah 53.

The relevant passage in Isaiah chapter 53 (verses 4-6) is full of the language of sin, of punishment and of substitution:

> Surely he has borne our griefs and carried our sorrows; yet we esteemed him stricken, smitten by God, and afflicted. But he was wounded for our transgressions; he was crushed for our iniquities; upon him was the chastisement that brought us peace, and with his stripes we are healed. All we like sheep have gone astray; we have turned – every one – to his own way; and the Lord has laid on him the iniquity of us all.

The language of sin and rebellion is contained in the words *'transgression'*, which speaks of wandering from God; *'iniquity'*, which speaks of falling short of God's standards; and *'turning to our own way'* rather than God's. The language of substitution is contained in the repeated insistence that it was not for his own sin that the servant was suffering, but for ours: *'he was wounded for our transgression; he was crushed for our iniquities; upon him was the chastisement that brought us peace'*. The language of punishment is contained in the words *'wounded'*, *'crushed'* and *'chastisement'*. Right up front, as Matthew announces the arrival of God's King, he insists that God's King will rescue God's people by paying the satisfactory price for our sin. The *fulfilment* of all of this is seen at the end of the gospel as we see Jesus hanging on the cross, being punished for our sin, in our place, so that we can walk free. The *anticipation* of this is found right at the start of Matthew's gospel as the angel tells Joseph:

> "you shall call his name Jesus, for he will save his people from their sins." (chapter 1 verse 21)

I love it that Matthew includes this foretaste of the cross right here in chapter 8 as he announces the arrival of God's King. It is highly likely that for the vast majority of us reading these words, our response to the matchless majesty of Jesus' character and to the perfect demands of his law is that of the Roman centurion in verse 8:

> "Lord, I am not worthy to have you come under my roof."

We have no idea what had gone on in this man's house, but as he considered Jesus' perfect character and absolute demand for holy living, he was quite clear that he fell far, far short of the perfection Jesus required. You might say, using the language of the Sermon on the Mount, that he saw that he was '*poor in spirit*'. It is this poverty of spirit – or rebellion against God – that is the cause, ultimately, of everything that is wrong with our fallen world. At the final count, it is our personal sin that cuts us off from our creator and demands his final judgment.

We have been reminded all too powerfully of this universal condition of humanity in these four scenes. However, we have also been shown God's glorious solution. Wherever we go across the globe, it is Jesus, God's King, who has come with all of God's authority to deal with death, the single most desperate fact of human existence. He has come to satisfy God's judgment at our sin through his death on the cross. As he pays the punishment for our rebellion, he satisfies God's just demands and enables us to walk free into a relationship of loving acceptance with God our

Father. Every one of us reading this chapter lies under the shadow or shroud of death and judgment. Jesus' authority and Jesus' offer extends to every one of us: he is God's long-awaited saviour.

Counting the Cost

In conclusion, then, how should we respond? We will have to wait until chapter 9 and verses 9-13 to see the model positive response that Jesus demands. For now, in chapter 8 verses 18-22, Matthew follows the quotation from Isaiah with two examples of inappropriate responses.

Two men came up to Jesus in quick succession, one a scribe, the other a disciple. The first offered too much too soon: *'Teacher, I will follow you wherever you go'*. He had not yet realised that Jesus is *'the Son of Man'*, with all God's authority over his kingdom; nor had he realised that Jesus was not only going to forgo his human rights, but even abandon the creature comforts that we assume normal for foxes and birds as he made his way selflessly to his sacrificial death. This first man warns us against promising to do too much too soon for Jesus; to follow him will mean total surrender to his authority, even as we benefit from the glorious promise of his new creation banquet.

The second man, described as a *'disciple'*, offered too little too late. Like many Christians today, he didn't see the urgency of what it was that Jesus had come to do and so he thought that he could simply tack his discipleship on to all the other seemingly important and vital priorities of the day. There can be no human responsibility that is greater for a man than to oversee the death and burial of his father. In demanding instant obedience, Jesus used a deliberately shocking teaching technique in order to emphasise the absolute priority of following him as we come under his kingdom rule. He had come to deal with all the effects of this fallen world as he ushered in his new heavenly kingdom through his death on the cross. Discipleship, for those who understand the times, will require radical action and a wholehearted response that puts following him ahead of every other priority and commitment in life.

Questions:

1. Do you think that suffering, sickness and death preoccupy us as much in our 21st century culture as they did in the 1st century? Why do you think we are so loath to talk about these things today?

2. Verses 1-17 are full of examples of the authority of Jesus. Over what does Jesus demonstrate his absolute authority and how is that authority shown? (Look up Numbers 12 verses 12-15 and 2 Kings 5 verse 7 for an understanding of leprosy).

3. Look up Isaiah 25 verses 6-9. These verses speak of God's promise of rescue from judgment for his people. What do we learn about the rescue that God has promised?

4. In what different ways do the events of Matthew 8 verses 1–17 fulfil the promises of Isaiah 25?

5. Turn to Matthew 11 verse 2-6. This is the start of the next major section of Matthew's gospel. What does Jesus tell us we should have learned from Matthew chapters 8–10?

6. How does chapter 8 verses 1-17 teach us these lessons?

7. Verse 17 is a quotation from Isaiah 53 verse 4-6. What does this suggest to us about how Jesus will accomplish the rescue that God promises?

8. What do we learn from each of the characters: the leper, the centurion, Peter's mother-in-law?

9. What mistake does the scribe of verse 19 make? What about the disciple of verse 21? How might we make the same mistake?

Preacher's Note 1

You will notice that I am making two assumptions here. The first is that Matthew treats Israel at the time of Jesus' arrival as if they are still experiencing the effects of the Exile. Although the people of Israel may have returned to the land under Ezra / Nehemiah, the effects of God's judgment are still being experienced in the land. This way of handling the material is consistent both with the muted end of Ezra / Nehemiah and with the introduction to Matthew's gospel. Chapter 1 verse 17 suggests that we are correct to read it this way: *'So all the generations from Abraham to David were fourteen generations, and from David to the deportation to Babylon fourteen generations, and from the deportation to Babylon to the Christ fourteen generations.'* Matthew does not mention the return to the land of Nehemiah's day. He skips straight to the coming of the Christ. The second assumption is that Israel and her exile exhibit in microcosm the pattern of humanity and the Fall. This explains why we have taken the lessons concerning God's judgment and salvation for Israel and applied them to all of humanity.

Preacher's Note 2

Following the ideas introduced in Preachers Note 1, you will notice that I have taken a Biblical Theological approach to sickness, death, and natural disasters, understanding them to be the result of human sin and God's judgment. The presence of these things in the Land of God's Promise makes them even more theologically offensive. Whilst this approach involves obvious pastoral 'risks', it is vital that we pursue it, for it enables us to make clear the impact of sin and its consequences in our world. Our world is fallen and the results of human sin and God's judgment are to be seen everywhere we look. Once we are bold enough to point out the effects of human sin in terms of sickness, death and disease, the universal need for a saviour becomes abundantly clear. Too often the evangelist is left searching for a 'hook' with which to 'make our gospel relevant' to his listeners. Once we tackle the reality of sin and its effects head on, the way Matthew does, there are 'hooks' everywhere; what is more, they are biblical 'hooks' and not the inappropriate hooks alluded to in 2 Corinthians 4 verse 2.

Preacher's Note 3

I am following the traditional understanding of the structure of Matthew's gospel, namely that he marks the divisions of each major section of his gospel with the concluding phrase: *'when Jesus had finished all these sayings'* (7:28; 11:1; 13:53; 19:1; 26:1). This structure suggests that there are five major sections to the gospel with a prologue in chapters 1 and 2 and a conclusion in chapters 26 to 28. Once we have grasped the key issue being addressed in each section, each one makes a 'preachable unit' and can be taken and used in appropriate circumstances. I tend to give each section a title and thus would argue that the gospel can be broken down as follows:

1:1 – 2:23	Prologue
3:1 – 7:29	Announcing the Kingdom
8:1 – 10:42	The arrival of the King
11:1 – 13:52	The advance of the Kingdom
13:53 – 18:35	Assembling the Kingdom
19:1 – 25:46	The authentic King
26:1 – 28:20	Conclusion

TWO

The   Arrival   of   the   King: Summoning Sinners

Matthew 8:23-9:13

And when he got into the boat, his disciples followed him. ²⁴And behold, there arose a great storm on the sea, so that the boat was being swamped by the waves; but he was asleep. ²⁵And they went and woke him, saying, "Save us, Lord; we are perishing." ²⁶And he said to them, "Why are you afraid, O you of little faith?" Then he rose and rebuked the winds and the sea, and there was a great calm. ²⁷And the men marvelled, saying, "What sort of man is this, that even winds and sea obey him?" ²⁸And when he came to the other side, to the country of the Gadarenes, two demon-possessed men met him, coming out of the tombs, so fierce that no one could pass that way. ²⁹And behold, they cried out, "What have you to do with us, O Son of God? Have you come here to torment us before the time?" ³⁰Now a herd of many pigs was feeding at some distance from them. ³¹And the demons begged him, saying, "If you cast us out, send us away into the herd of pigs." ³²And he said to them, "Go." So they came out and went into the pigs, and behold, the whole herd rushed down the steep bank into the sea and drowned in the waters. [33]The herdsmen fled, and going into the city they told everything, especially what had happened to the demon-possessed men. [34]And behold, all the city came out to meet Jesus, and when they saw him, they begged him to leave their region.

[9:1]And getting into a boat he crossed over and came to his own city. [2]And behold, some people brought to him a paralytic, lying on a bed. And when Jesus saw their faith, he said to the paralytic, "Take heart, my son; your sins are forgiven." [3]And behold, some of the scribes said to themselves, "This man is blaspheming." [4]But Jesus, knowing their thoughts, said, "Why do you think evil in your hearts? [5]For which is easier, to say, 'Your sins are forgiven,' or to say, 'Rise and walk'? [6]But that you may know that the Son of Man has authority on earth to forgive sins"- he then said to the paralytic- "Rise, pick up your bed and go home." [7]And he rose and went home. [8]When the crowds saw it, they were afraid, and they glorified God, who had given such authority to men. [9]As Jesus passed on from there, he saw a man called Matthew sitting at the tax booth, and he said to him, "Follow me." And he rose and followed him. [10]And as Jesus reclined at table in the house, behold, many tax collectors and sinners came and were reclining with Jesus and his disciples. [11]And when the Pharisees saw this, they said to his disciples, "Why does your teacher eat with tax collectors and sinners?" [12]But when he heard it, he said, "Those who are well have no need of a physician, but those who are sick. [13]Go and learn what this means, 'I desire mercy, and not sacrifice.' For I came not to call the righteous, but sinners."

On New Year's Eve 2007, one of the British weekend news magazines carried a front-page picture of our world. The picture was taken from outer space, and superimposed above the picture of the globe was another image, George Bush and Tony Blair. They had their backs to the world, and they were walking away from it. George Bush had one arm around Tony Blair's shoulder. At the centre of the picture, right the way across the middle of the world, was a huge sticking-plaster and blood was oozing out from under it. Anyone who has ever read any of Bush and Blair's early foreign policy speeches will realise just how damning a picture it is. Theirs was to be a new global order, and the new global village was going to enable free trade, the expansion of wealth and the eradication of poverty. With just a little imagination, we could write the rest of the speech ourselves! Indeed, one of Blair's own cabinet members wrote an article in the earliest months of his premiership entitled, 'How we will build the New Jerusalem'[1]. After ten years, the image in the New Year magazine said it all: our world bleeds on.

Of course, Bush and Blair aren't the only ones to have offered sticking-plaster solutions to the world. I recently came across a new edition of the Communist Party Manifesto, first published in English in 1848. Marx and Engels dreamed dreams too:

> As the exploitation of one individual by another is put to an end, so the exploitation of one nation by another will also be put to an end. As the antagonism between classes within the nations vanish, so the hostility of one nation to another will come to an end.[2]

The bloody and violent failure of the Communist utopian dream is even more devastating than the bloody and violent failure of the capitalist one. Just think of the Soviet Union, China and Cambodia, and all the wickedness that was perpetrated under Stalin, Mao and Pol Pot.

It's not just the capitalists or the Communists. *The Second Humanist Manifesto* of 1973 reads:

---

[1] Patricia Hewitt on Frank Field's welfare reform Green Paper in *The Times*, 25 March 1998.

[2] *The Communist Manifesto* 1848 Karl Marx and Friedrich Engels. This edition 1998 page 58 Published by Verso.

By using technology wisely, we will control our environment, conquer poverty, modify human behaviour, alter the course of human evolution and cultural development, and provide humankind with an unparalleled opportunity for achieving an abundant and meaningful life.[3]

If the arrogance of the vision were not so unpalatable, it would almost be comic!

Of course, our desire for a saviour for our world is not a bad or a wrong thing, is it? We would have to be blind or utterly heartless not to realize that our world needs a saviour and to long for one. Whether it's poverty, drought, climate change, disease, natural catastrophe or personal tragedy, our world bleeds. Therefore it is a quite natural and compassionate thing for us to cry out, 'Make poverty history!' 'Give peace a chance!' 'Feed the world!' The trouble is, we have been offered so many band-aids that have failed and that don't go to the heart of the problem that we have grown weary and cynical about calls to action. Meanwhile, the world bleeds on.

Matthew's aim in chapters 8–10 is to show us that Jesus Christ is the King who has arrived as God's Saviour for our broken world. We can be sure that this is the issue that Matthew is focused on, because at the start of the third section of his gospel, Matthew summarises the key point of the chapters we are studying by recording John the Baptist's question to Jesus: '*Are you the one who is to come, or shall we look for another?*' (11 verse 3). In reply, Jesus goes back over the events of chapters 8–10 in order to demonstrate that he is the one to come, the Saviour of the world, with all the necessary power and authority. We can conclude, therefore, that the Bible itself tells us that we are right to long for a saviour. John the Baptist was looking for the Saviour who was to come, and

---

[3] This can be found on the Web. It is worth reading the full text with its 17 articles.

this section of the gospel demonstrates that indeed the Saviour has arrived. So then the aim of this second study is for us to see that Jesus is not just another sticking-plaster solution, but that the salvation he has come to bring goes right to the heart of the problem of our world because it goes right to the heart of every human being.

As we come face to face with the true Jesus of history, we should find ourselves becoming more deeply aware of the wonder and glory of Jesus. It was the Russian author Dostoevsky who wrote:

> I believe that there is no one lovelier, no one better, no one more sympathetic and more perfect than Jesus. I say to myself with jealous love that not only is there no one else like him, but that there never could be anybody else like him.[4]

There could be few more appropriate responses to a study of this passage.

Jesus as Lord of Creation

Just as the themes of death, disease and sickness in the first seventeen verses of chapter 8 show us men and women experiencing the effects of living in a fallen world, so the storm in verses 23-27 presents us with the picture of an ungovernable world out of relationship with its creator, under the judgment of God, with the very elements of creation groaning and rising up in rebellion against the Lord. By calming the storm, Jesus shows that he is the one with the power to rescue and restore this created order.

In order to gain a better understanding of what is going on in these verses, we need to take a step backwards and spend some time considering Adam and Eve's fall and its impact on our world

---

[4] Quoted in *Is Anyone There?* p. 40. David Coulson, Hodder Christian Paperbacks.

order, which is recorded in Genesis chapter 3. (See Preacher's Notes 1 and 2 from chapter 1) Their rebellion against God's loving rule affected far more than simply their own individual relationship with God. Since humankind had been given such a pivotal role as the lynchpin of God's governance over God's world (Genesis 1:28), their rejection of the creator impacted the whole of the physical created order over which God had given them delegated authority. Since the day of humanity's original rebellion, the whole physical world has been under God's judgment, even as each human being has continued to repeat the rebellion in each individual life. Elsewhere in Matthew's Gospel, Jesus speaks of uprisings of '*kingdom against kingdom*' and of '*famines and earthquakes in various places*' and he says '*these are but the beginning of the birth pains*', by which he means that the physical world is experiencing the birth-pangs of God's judgment today (Matthew 24 verses 7-8). The Apostle Paul speaks of creation '*groaning together in the pains of childbirth*' (Romans 8 verse 22). To use the image of the Sunday magazine supplement, our world is bleeding.

Somebody once used the illustration of shattered glass to explain the impact of our rebellion and God's judgment on creation. If you have ever had the misfortune to break a window or a windscreen, you will know how what seems to be the smallest impact causes cracks and splinters to extend right the way across the pane. I remember once shaking out a duvet the morning after staying in a friend's house. To my horror, as I shook out the bed-cover, a coin was sent spinning across the room to the centre of a full-length antique mirror. There was a sharp crack as it hit and then fissures ran right across the glass to the edges of the frame. It was not a happy breakfast! That is a good illustration of the extent of the damage caused by the fall of humanity. As mankind rejected the loving rule of our Lord and creator, so the effect of that rebellion and his judgment spread to the deepest recesses of the created order. God's judgment is still experienced not only in sin, disease and death, but also in the groaning of our world.

This storm at sea in verses 23-27 of chapter 8 is a classic example of the created order joining in the rebellion of humanity against the creator. The disciples provide a perfect example of our helplessness in the wake of the whirlwind that was sown by human rebellion. These disciples were hardened fishermen – the Sea of Galilee was their office! – yet that day as they arrived in the office, they found themselves totally out of their depth.

> And behold, there arose a great storm on the sea, so that the boat was being swamped by the waves; but he was asleep. And they went and woke him, saying, "Save us, Lord; we are perishing."

The purpose of these verses is to show us that Jesus Christ, who has come in all of God's majesty to restore and rule his new creation, really is Lord. Jesus' response shows his absolute authority as God's King come to rescue.

> And he said to them, "Why are you afraid, O you of little faith?" Then he rose and rebuked the winds and the sea, and there was a great calm.

Only God can do the sort of thing that Jesus did that day. With just a word, he spoke and the uncontrollable elements of our created order were subdued.

One of my favourite places on earth is a bay in the South West of England. It looks out across the Atlantic, with no land between the coast of Cornwall and the East coast of America. I was walking there at Christmas time, shortly after there had been a massive storm at sea. The sea was raging and the waves towered over my head as they crashed down on the rocks. I knew I was due to speak on this section of Matthew's Gospel a few days later, and so I went behind one of the rocks whilst no-one was listening or watching and shouted at the waves: 'Be still!' You can imagine the results! Fortunately, my pathetic shouts were drowned out by the continued crashing of the waves and nobody noticed what was going on! The disciples knew that only God can do the kind of thing Jesus did that day as he showed his absolute divine authority over this created order even as it rebelled against his rightful rule. Their response was entirely appropriate:

> And the men marvelled, saying, "What sort of man is this, that even winds and sea obey him?"

It is as if Jesus had been standing on the beaches of a Thai holiday resort on Boxing Day 2004, or on the levees in New Orleans with hurricane Katrina approaching, or in Burma as the typhoon raged, and at his word the winds and waves had abated. It is impossible to miss the point. Jesus is the long-awaited Saviour who has all of God's authority over all of God's created order. He is the one who was expected to come, and with the calming of the storm it is as if he says to us that we need look no further.

There can be no doubt that we live in a world where the physical order of creation has been impacted by our human rebellion and God's subsequent judgment, but Jesus has come with all of God's majesty as the Lord who is able to bring about God's perfect new creation.

Jesus as the Destroyer of Evil

The encounter with the demon-possessed men demonstrates that Jesus has all of God's power ultimately to destroy and wipe out all evil. Just as the storm is an example of our fallen created world, so the two demon-possessed men are models of the destructive and dehumanizing work of Satan. It seems that they did not have what we could call mental illness, for elsewhere Matthew distinguishes between epilepsy and demon-possession (chapter 4 verse 24). Rather they are at the extreme end of Satan's influence on a human's life. We can see that simply by glancing at verse 28:

> When he came to the other side, to the country of the Gadarenes, two demon-possessed men met him, coming out of the tombs, so fierce that no one could pass that way.

These men had been rendered so violent and dehumanized that no-one was able to pass; they lived in the place of the dead, the tombs, which means that they had been rendered spiritually unclean. People were so terrified of them that they deliberately diverted their path rather than pass through the region, indeed the area had been made into a no-go zone. We can imagine these men emerging from their morbid abode with hair bedraggled, clothes torn, teeth broken and black, and with spit and scraps of last week's food dribbling down their beards. Not only were they visually terrifying, but they were also totally out of control. Amazingly, however, as these men came to Jesus, they recognised him for who he was and addressed him as God's King, using the title '*Son of God*', which is another name for God's long-awaited Messiah (see Psalm 2). Then these uncontrollable tearaways, who had the whole region in their devilish grip, begged Jesus that he might leave them alone:

> the demons begged him, saying, "If you cast us out, send us away into the herd of pigs."

Once again the point is obvious: Jesus has come as God's King with all of God's power to destroy evil.

When the Bible speaks of Satan, it is not talking about a comic character wearing red tights with pointy horns; nor does it have in mind a fairy-tale figure such as Harry Potter's 'He-Who-Shall-Not-Be-Named'. Satan, the devil, is the personal force for evil who lies behind all rebellion against God in this world. We would have to be remarkably naïve not to believe in such a figure. After the First Gulf War, Bernard Levin, a famous British columnist, wrote an article in *The Times* on the devil. He argued that our repeated failure to wipe out evil shows the folly and naivety of those who have bought the lie that Satan does not exist. The final line of his article read:

> We don't believe in the devil, do we? The trouble is, the devil does believe in us.[5]

Just recently I came across Joachim Fest's account of the last day of Hitler's Reich in the bunker.[6] When we read of or hear about the atrocities of an Adolf Hitler, or of the recent revelations of Josef Fritzl who kept his daughter locked in a cellar in order to continue his incestuous relationship with her, it is hard not to conclude that such evil is beyond the influence simply of *the World* and *the Flesh*.

Once we face up to the fact of the existence of the devil, we would have to be extremely warped not to long for the destruction of evil. Indeed, without the destruction of evil, we can propose one after another remedy for solving the problems of humanity and our world, but ultimately they will only ever be sticking-plaster solutions. Over and again our remedies will be thwarted because of the wickedness of human rebellion, led on under the power of Satan.

I am of the generation that used to belt out at the top of my voice John Lennon's *Imagine*. It's a great song and I suspect that most of us, if we are over 40 and under 70, will have succumbed to our own personal karaoke, even if only in the privacy of our shower! Some of the lyrics express a deep longing:

> *Imagine all the people living for today.*
> *Imagine all the people living life in peace.*

---

[5] 'Satan laughs at Yugoslavia', 18 September 1991.
[6] *Inside Hitler's Bunker* by Joachim C Fest, published by Macmillan.

Imagine all the people sharing all the world.
I hope some day you'll join us, and the world will live as one.

However, Lennon's longing is, and only ever can be, a figment of the imagination. For there can be 'no brotherhood of man' without the destruction and removal of wickedness; there can be no 'living life in peace' without the purification and cleansing of all that opposes God; and there can be no 'sharing of the world' without the disarming of all evil and its right, just and measured punishment. Therefore Lennon, together with Lenin and all utopian dreamers, whether secularists, capitalists or liberal humanists, can only ever ask us simply to 'imagine', for they have no answer to the destructive power of evil. Their solutions will only ever be of the band-aid variety as our world bleeds on.

Before we can feed the world, or give peace a chance, or make poverty history, or save the planet, there simply has to be someone who, in the language of Psalm 2, '*shall break [God's enemies] with a rod of iron and dash them in pieces like a potter's vessel*' (Psalm 2 verse 9). The command of Jesus to the demon-possessed men in verse 32 shows us that Jesus is that man. Not only has he come as Lord in majesty to rule God's new creation, he has come as King, the Son of God, with all of God's power to destroy, once and for all, all of God's enemies:

And he said to them, "Go." So they came out and went into the pigs.

There is no incantation, no ceremony, no exorcism, no asking for God's help, no bell, book and candle. With a simple word of command the demons, like the wind and waves before them, do his bidding.

Before we move on to chapter 9, it is important that we pause and notice one key phrase in verse 29 which we might all too easily skip over. In their response to Jesus, the demons tell us something very important about the time-frame of Christ's kingdom rule, enabling us to have a clear grasp of the times in which we live:

> And behold, they cried out, "What have you to do with us, O Son of God? Have you come here to torment us *before the time*?"

It seems that the demons had realized that Jesus had not come *yet* to destroy them, which is why they asked him simply to cast them out into the pigs. It is as if they saw that Jesus will come *one day* finally to destroy them, just as Psalm 2 tells us he will, but for then it was as if he had come 'early', before the appointed time. As Jesus drove them out to continue their devilish work in the herd of pigs, he demonstrated that he has all of God's power as God's King utterly to destroy evil once and for all and to rid this world order of all that is evil. However, the recognition by the demons that Jesus had come in advance of that final day, enables us to see that he has not come *yet* to bring about the final destruction of all evil.

Grasping this point about the time-frame of Christ's kingdom helps us to answer one of the big puzzles concerning Jesus' kingly rule. Sometimes a person will respond to all that we are seeing in these few chapters of Matthew's gospel by saying something like this: 'If Jesus really does have all this authority, then why wasn't Jesus there on the banks of the Mississippi during the hurricane, or in Burma at the time of the typhoon, or Thailand when the tsunami struck?' The answer is that one day he will step in again, and all that spoils this world will be brought to an end: the raging storms will cease, all evil will be destroyed, and Jesus' kingdom rule will be established on earth forever. However, as Jesus walked the earth, it was as if he gave us an advance viewing of his new creation under his perfect rule. This is how it is that we Christians can say with confidence that our vision of the future is not a 'pie-in-the-sky-when-you-die' fantasy. Unlike the utopian dreams of the Marxist or humanist, the certainty of Jesus' second coming is rooted in the historical reality of Jesus' first coming. In his first coming, he gave us clear evidence both of who he is and of what his rule will ultimately be like. Sometimes people ask me what heaven will be like. I always reply: 'look at Jesus when he walked the earth, it will be that glorious, and better!'

I live in a part of London where people always seem to be knocking down old buildings and putting up new ones. Having lived in our area for some time now, I have spotted a recognisable pattern to the way the developers work. They begin with the demolition of the old structure. Once the demolition has started, a wooden barrier is erected all around the outside of the site in order to prevent access. Within just a matter of weeks, a sign appears saying: 'New flats coming soon. Show home available for advance viewing.' At that point, even though the site is still filled with rubble and debris of the old order, it is possible to walk behind the wooden fence, through a carefully prepared corridor and into a new flat, in pristine condition. For the potential purchaser, it provides a snap-shot of the future that the developers are bringing into being.[7]

As Jesus walked the earth, God's Lord appeared in all his majesty. He is God's King, with all of God's authority, and in his life and work we are given a glimpse of the certain future that he will bring into being on the day he speaks his powerful word of command, summoning the elements to order and condemning Satan and all his forces to destruction. He has come as King with all of God's power to destroy evil.

Jesus as Forgiving Judge

Once we realise that Jesus came early, before the appointed time, it leaves us asking the obvious question: 'what on earth, then, did

---

[7] Like all the best illustrations this one has been stolen (from Nigel Beynon who used it first one Sunday night at St Helen's.)

Jesus come to do?' That is exactly the question Matthew goes on to address in chapter 9 verses 1-7. (Preacher's note 1) One of the things I love about Matthew's gospel is his relentless logic. He has all the ordered structure and logical clarity of a tax-collecting money-man!

In chapter 9 verses 1-7, Jesus gives himself another new title. He has already been called 'Lord' (8 verse 25) and 'Son of God' (8 verse 29), both of which are titles used in the Old Testament for God's long-awaited King (see for example Psalm 110 verse 1 and Psalm 2 verse 7). Now, in chapter 9 verse 6, Jesus calls himself 'the Son of Man'. Once again this is a title for God's King. It carries connotations of the final judgment of all humanity. In the Old Testament it occurs in the book of Daniel chapter 7, where the Son of Man is given dominion and glory and a kingdom, and peoples of all nations worship him in his kingdom, which is a kingdom that goes on from everlasting to everlasting (see verses 13-14).

However, we still need to answer the question: 'why has the Son of Man, God's judge, come to earth early?' The answer is in Jesus' command to the paralytic who has been brought to him by his friends:

"But that you may know that the Son of Man has authority on earth to forgive sins" – he then said to the paralytic – "Rise, pick up your bed and go home."

Jesus is the judge who has come early with all of God's authority to forgive sins; he's not into temporary solutions. He has come to get right to the heart of the issue, by dealing with the problem of the human heart. One day he will come to overthrow all that spoils this world order and to provide his perfect new creation for his people, but in order for his people to be ready for that day, he has come early to forgive sins.

There is no doubt that Jesus' opening remark to the paralytic ranks as one of the most politically incorrect things ever said. It is almost impossible to imagine anybody speaking as Jesus did to the paralysed man:

> Behold, some people brought to him a paralytic, lying on a bed. And when Jesus saw their faith, he said to the paralytic, "Take heart, my son; your sins are forgiven."

The only possible justification for such a statement would be if the forgiveness of the paralytic's sins was in reality a far greater need and priority than the healing of his sickness. As we pause to consider who Jesus is, we have to conclude that Jesus' prioritising of this mans's need for forgiveness does indeed pinpoint his greatest need. For if Jesus is Lord with all of God's majesty, who will bring into being God's new creation; and if Jesus is King with all of God's power to destroy evil; and if Jesus has come to establish his glorious new heaven and earth, of which these verses give us an advance viewing; and if he is the Son of Man who will judge every man and woman who has ever lived, then forgiveness by him of all our sins is surely the top priority that any individual ever has to face.

Picture a packed football stadium, or a crowded underground carriage, or the busy streets in a great humming metropolis – over and again we could settle our gaze on one individual after another and pose the question: 'what is this individual's greatest need for all eternity?' No matter how often you shift your gaze from one person to another, the answer will always be the same: 'the forgiveness of sin.'

As Jesus claimed to offer forgiveness and to deal with the paralytic's most pressing concern, the theologically-attuned scribes were only too clear what was going on. They could see that Jesus was claiming to do the thing that God alone has authority to do and so they objected, '*this man is blaspheming*'. In order to highlight to the scribes who he was and what authority he had been given as '*the Son of Man*', Jesus posed a tough question which is not at all easy to answer. For many years I thought that it was easier to say, *'your sins are forgiven'* than to say, *'rise, pick up your bed and go home.'* After all, if I simply say, *'your sins are forgiven,'* no-one can actually see whether what I have said has been achieved. However, we need to remember that Jesus was speaking to the scribes here. They had already pointed out that God *alone* can say *'your sins are forgiven'* – no human being has the right to say such a thing. They thought it was both humanly wrong to say and humanly impossible to do such a thing. Equally, though, we have to agree that it is humanly impossible to say: *'Rise, pick up your bed and go home.'* Just as no human being can control the storm or destroy evil, so no human being can heal a life-long paralytic with just a word. So the answer to Jesus' question, *'which is easier to say'*, is that *both* things are equally impossible for a human to say and do – we have here two impossible things! Therefore, in order to demonstrate that he really had the power to do the things that God alone can do, and had come with all of God's authority to *say* the humanly impossible, Jesus spoke a word to the paralytic and *did* the humanly impossible.

I once asked a medic what it would have meant for this paralysed man to get up, pick up his mat and walk. He said to me, 'William, have you ever broken a limb?' Yes, a leg. I was in plaster for 12 weeks. 'What was it like when the plaster came off?' Why, the leg was absolutely shrivelled. The muscles were shot to bits. In fact, it took a full 12 months of physiotherapy and extensive exercise before I reached the peak of physical fitness in which you would find me today! Apparently, with long-term paralysis, there is the additional complication of joints contracting as the muscles wither. As the joints contract, the limbs are dragged out of line in what is known as 'contractures'. It would therefore be impossible simply to speak and then, without physiotherapy and endless joint-restoring muscular exercise, for a person to stand, let alone for him to pick up his bed and walk home! In order to demonstrate that he had the power to say the impossible thing –*'your sins are forgiven'* – Jesus, with just a word, spoke and did the impossible thing. And what happened? The paralytic *'rose and went home.'* I like to think that he jumped up and danced home, singing and shouting for all he was worth! However, Matthew doesn't dwell on that, because he wants us to grasp his main point that Jesus, the Son of Man, had come early, with all of God's supreme authority as judge, in order to offer his people the forgiveness of their sins. When the crowd saw what happened, they realised the implications of what was going on: *'they were afraid, and they glorified God, who had given such authority to men.'*

This story enables us to come to a much clearer understanding of the times in which we live. Jesus came to do far more than simply apply sticking-plasters to our world, he was not into band-aid solutions. He came as the one who will rule over God's new creation with all of God's majesty, he is the Lord. Jesus came as the one with all of God's power to destroy evil utterly, he is the Son of God (God's King). Also, he came *early* to get right to the heart of the problem – the problem of the human heart. He is the Son of Man, God's final judge of all, but he came before the appointed time with all of God's authority on earth to forgive sins and bring his people into a right relationship with God.

It is as if God has a diary, and on the final page is the day when what the demons are anticipating in verse 29 will happen, when they will be destroyed utterly and all the effects of human rebellion against God will be dealt with. On that day, Jesus will usher in a whole new world order. We will never wake up again to a tsunami, there will never again be an earthquake, or a famine, or a war. There will be no sickness, no sadness, no tears, no suffering. This is the day at the end of all time that is yet to come. However, Jesus came early. He came in his grace and mercy and divine humility, and he entered into the heart of his creation as the Son of Man, the Lord and judge, to go to the cross, to carry God's judgment on sin, to take on himself all of our rebellion and wickedness, so that he might enable us to be reunited with our creator in a restored relationship and so that he might clothe us and fit us for a place in his glorious new creation. We live in between the times of his first and second comings, a time when his offer of grace and forgiveness is open to all who will turn and obey his command to follow him, as Matthew himself had done. These, then, are the times in which we live.

Jesus as the Friend of Sinners

Once again, with the glorious logic of the tax man, Matthew takes us straight on to our next point. (Preacher's note 2)

> As Jesus passed on from there, he saw a man called Matthew (the writer of this gospel) sitting at the tax booth, and he said to him, "Follow me." And he rose and followed him.

Notice, it is not Matthew who chose Jesus. Jesus summoned Matthew! The action in verses 9-13 was at Jesus' initiative, but Matthew obeyed. Matthew goes on to tell us of the banquet that was laid on in honour of Jesus back at his house. This shows us that the messianic banquet at the end of time (about which we heard in chapter 8 verse 11 when Jesus was speaking about the centurion, and which we will read of in chapter 9 verses 14-17) is a feast to which sinners will be welcomed as they come from east and west in obedience to Jesus' command: *'follow me'*.

It is important to realise that whilst Matthew might have been godless, he certainly wasn't friendless. Sometimes, when people speak of the tax collectors in the first century, they paint them as oddballs and social outcasts. That certainly was not the case with Matthew! As a tax collector, he was a *religious* outcast. He had deliberately sided with the occupying Roman forces, and as a tax collector he was part of that notorious band whose dishonest practices and ruthless oppression were directed against their own countrymen, the people of Israel. So Matthew was certainly not a God-fearer, quite the reverse. However, we would be wrong to paint him as a social misfit. He may have been rejected by the religious establishment, but he did have friends – many of them – and his friendship group was made up of godless rebels like him who were known as '*sinners*'.

In understanding who Matthew represents today, then, we need to think of a person whom we would least expect ever to see in church; the most unlikely relative, the person in our workplace whom we would least expect to see at a Christian meeting, an out-and-out spiritual outcast, a man or woman who knows nothing of God and has lived a life of brazen rebellion against him. Matthew would have been today's equivalent of the atheist or agnostic with little or no moral conscience. He may be the equivalent of somebody from the upper reaches of the establishment, an MP, perhaps, even a Cabinet minister; or somebody who has been reported in the press for something terrible that they have done; or he may be an ordinary, unknown, everyday rebel against God who wants nothing whatsoever to do with God or with God's people. That evening, because the time had come to summon sinners, Jesus gathered '*sinners*' around him and he '*reclined at table*' with them.

I like to call this little incident 'the party that rocked the religious,' because this is the sort of thing the religious hate. Religion is really just another human solution alongside capitalism and socialism and secularism. As we in the West witness the failure of the atheistic alternatives to religion (with which we experimented with such self-destructive enthusiasm in the twentieth century), it is almost certain we shall see a return to the man-made solution of religion. It is important that we grasp that religion has precisely the same shortcomings, for it too seeks to apply short-term solutions to the problems of our world by giving us religious rules and regulations to obey, rather than dealing with the heart of the problems of the world that flow, ultimately, from the problems of the human heart. The religious always create a club where those on the inside have badges of belonging and codes of conduct that enable them to mark themselves up and others down. That's why Jesus described them in verse 13 as '*the righteous'*. It wasn't that they were perfect – far from it! Rather, the religious are the self-congratulating, smugly self-satisfied who think that they are spiritually well.

This explains why the Pharisees responded with such disapproval in verse 11:

> And when the Pharisees saw this, they said to his disciples, "Why does your teacher eat with tax collectors and sinners?"

Jesus was quick to deal with their objection, for as the perfect divine physician he had come to deal with those who recognised that they were spiritually diseased. Whilst the smugly self-satisfied want nothing to do with Jesus because he breaks all the rules of their club, the *'sinners'* flock to him, because he alone can deal with their greatest need. The irony is that, like the cancer patient in denial, the religious are as equally in need of his healing care as the *'sinners'*.

Conclusion

The aim of this chapter has been to show us that Jesus Christ is the one who has come as God's Saviour for our broken world. I said as we started that we should finish the chapter with our delight in Jesus refreshed. Remember Dostoevsky's assessment of Jesus: 'I say to myself with jealous love that not only is there no one else like him, but there never could be anybody like him.' We have considered the matchless majesty of Jesus, he came as Lord; we have witnessed the powerful divinity of Jesus, he came as King; we have seen the authoritative humility of Jesus, he came early to go to a cross to forgive sinners. We have noticed the compassionate mercy of Jesus, and discovered that he came to summon sinners. We have learned of the radical new kingdom of Jesus and that he came to usher in a new day for God's forgiven people in his new covenant community

In conclusion, we should notice what it will look like for a person to line up with the one who is to come.

First, from the calming of the storm we learn that we can live in faith, not in fear. Jesus says to his disciples, '*Why are you so afraid, O you of little faith?*' Many people I know live life plagued by a sense of fear. Some are fearful at the possibility of climate change, others fear for their loved ones; yet others live life overshadowed by fear for their own safety. Some have irrational fears about the future, whilst some parents are so full of fear that they become stiflingly protective of their children. Once we have seen the matchless majesty of Jesus Christ, who is both Lord of this creation and will effortlessly usher in his new creation, then we can live by faith, trusting that if he is with us, then we need not fear. The Psalmist has this conviction and demonstrates it in abundance in Psalm 91.

> He who dwells in the shelter of the Most High
> will abide in the shadow of the Almighty.
> I will say to the LORD, "My refuge and my fortress,
> my God, in whom I trust."

Secondly, from the incident with the demoniacs we learn that we can give ourselves to people rather than to pigs. In chapter 8 verse 33, we see an extraordinary thing happen. As the herdsmen fled from the scene of the healing, they raced into the city and told everything that had happened. Matthew notes carefully that they told '*everything, especially what had happened to the demon-possessed men.*' No doubt the cousins, uncles, aunts, parents, brothers and sisters of these demon-possessed men were living in that town. We might imagine that the people would have gone out from the town and said to Jesus, 'Fantastic! Come in! There's so much else that you can do!' However, Matthew notes carefully that, just as the demons had done, the townspeople *'begged him to leave.'* It seems that their priority and concern was for the status quo, for their money, for their well-being, for their quiet life. It can not be far wrong to suggest that they were more concerned about pigs than people. As we come to Jesus in his matchless majesty and powerful divinity, we can afford now to start living for people rather than for life as represented by those pigs!

Thirdly, we can afford to live glorying in God's goodness rather than grumbling at God. It is possible in the Christian life to enter into a dangerous pattern of grumbling at God, as we see the religious leaders doing in chapter 9 verses 1-8. Again, we would expect them to have been full of delight that at last the Son of Man had come, and that he had come with all God's authority to forgive sins. Instead they were more preoccupied with their theological objections to his identity and his work than with the person of Jesus and the wonder of his merciful ministry. 'I say to myself with jealous love that not only is there no one else like him, but there never could be.'

Suggested Questions for group or personal study

1. In what ways do our politicians, philosophers and public figures express our culture's longing that this world should be a better place?

2. Jesus demonstrates his authority in a number of ways in this passage. What are they? (For a better understanding of 8:23-27 look up Psalm 33:6-9).

3. What are the different titles that Jesus is given in this section? How do they fit with the question John the Baptist asks his disciples in 11:3?

4. What is it that the demons acknowledge about Jesus in 8:28-34? How do Jesus' subsequent actions show that their

statement is accurate? What does their phrase *'before the time'* tell us about Jesus' coming to the earth?

5. Why is the reaction of the people in the city so disturbing (8:34)? Why do they respond like this? How might we do the same?

6. Jesus' statement to the paralytic in 9:2 is highly politically incorrect. What does this tell us about Jesus' analysis of the man's real need? What does this say about Jesus' analysis of our greatest need?

7. What is the answer to Jesus' question in verse 5? Why has Jesus come to this earth *'before the time'*?

8. Why are the two reactions to Jesus in 9:1-7 so understandable?

9. Why are verses 9-13 such a logical next step after 9:1-7?

10. Go back through the whole section. What are the different reactions to Jesus? How and why might we react in the same way? Where the reactions are clearly wrong, why are they wrong and why should we react differently?

Preacher's Note 1

The way Matthew has laid out his material in this section demonstrates an immense level of care and attention to detail. Where he records the same incidents as Mark and Luke, Matthew usually does so with greater brevity. Matthew also leaves out lots of material that he could have put in. This shows that Matthew is working as a skilled theologian and that, commissioned and trained by Jesus, he is giving us an authoritative interpretation of Jesus' life and teaching. As we work through the section, please note the intense care that Matthew has taken with the placing of every verse. Over and again you will find that the more carefully we study the passages, the more we will be shown the precise reason why each part is phrased as it is and placed where it is. If we had time and space, I believe we could demonstrate that this whole section works as a giant sandwich, with the centre point being the section dealing with the demon-possessed men. The outer brackets of the chapters begin and end with the leper and the blind men; then come the two rulers (the centurion and the synagogue ruler); then the two women (Peter's mother-in-law and the woman with bleeding); then two theological statements as to who Jesus is and what he has come for; then two incidents of people who seek to 'follow Jesus', one false (the two men), the other genuine (Matthew); finally the storm is calmed and the paralytic is healed. The demon-possessed men stand in the centre of the section, showing us that Jesus has come early with authority over evil: hence the title of this book *Understanding the Times*. As preachers, our task is to work out not only what Matthew is telling us, but also why he is saying it this way and in this place. As we do so, we shall discover not only what his key theological points are, but also what is his God-given applicatory purpose. Under God, preaching that achieves this end will be powerful and will come with all of the authority of God's Holy Spirit.

Preacher's Note 2

We shall see this logic emerging repeatedly in our studies. In my view, as we discover the careful ordering of the Scriptures under the inspiration of God's Spirit, at least four ends will be attained. First, compelling sermons will be produced that carry the weighty authority of the text of Scripture itself. We will sense that this is God speaking as we discover the purpose he is aiming at. Second, it provides one of the most profound arguments for the authority of Scripture. The unlocking of the text makes the Scriptures self-authenticating as we hear the voice of God and see the hand of God in his word. Third, it trains congregational members for their own personal Bible study and gives them a hunger and desire to read the Bible in order to hear God speak. Fourth, it safeguards congregations against the activities of proof-texting by false teachers. These four considerations alone provide a powerful argument in favour of systematic expository preaching as the basic bread-and-butter of any congregation's diet. Preaching expository sermons requires immense and intense dependent work on the part of the preacher. Prayerful preparation needs to be started long in advance of the 'deadline' if we are to begin to see the pattern and ordered purpose of God in his word, and thus hear his voice. Rarely is a successful sermon begun at only 48 hours notice! The rewards of dependent hard work are immense, and the four I have listed are just a few of them.

Preacher's Note 3

You will notice that I have taken these two chapters in huge chunks! This is not something I would do in a sermon series at St Helen's or in a set of Bible studies. Indeed, we have run several series in chapters 8 and 9 dealing with each individual incident one at a time. This enables us to explore in far greater depth some of the issues of our fallen world that are raised by each sub-section and to root them in the equivalent experience of the Fall in 21st century England. I would recommend this. However, as we work through the two narrative chapters in a series of 8 or 10 sermons we need to keep the big picture clear. The aim of this section is for us to see that Jesus has arrived as God's King with all of God's authority, that he has come early to deal with sin and summon sinners, and that this first coming provides us with an eschatological window on what the future holds. As we keep this big picture in mind so the chapters will prove to be powerfully evangelistic and deeply edifying.

THREE

The Arrival of the King: Commanding Faith

Matthew 9:14-34

[14]Then the disciples of John came to him, saying, "Why do we and the Pharisees fast, but your disciples do not fast?" [15]And Jesus said to them, "Can the wedding guests mourn as long as the bridegroom is with them? The days will come when the bridegroom is taken away from them, and then they will fast. [16]No one puts a piece of unshrunk cloth on an old garment, for the patch tears away from the garment, and a worse tear is made. [17]Neither is new wine put into old wineskins. If it is, the skins burst and the wine is spilled and the skins are destroyed. But new wine is put into fresh wineskins, and so both are preserved." [18]While he was saying these things to them, behold, a ruler came in and knelt before him, saying, "My daughter has just died, but come and lay your hand on her, and she will live." [19] And Jesus rose and followed him, with his disciples. [20]And behold, a woman who had suffered from a discharge of blood for twelve years came up behind him and touched the fringe of his garment, [21]for she said to

herself, "If I only touch his garment, I will be made well." [22]Jesus turned, and seeing her he said, "Take heart, daughter; your faith has made you well." And instantly the woman was made well. [23]And when Jesus came to the ruler's house and saw the flute players and the crowd making a commotion, [24]he said, "Go away, for the girl is not dead but sleeping." And they laughed at him. [25]But when the crowd had been put outside, he went in and took her by the hand, and the girl arose. [26]And the report of this went through all that district. [27]And as Jesus passed on from there, two blind men followed him, crying aloud, "Have mercy on us, Son of David." [28]When he entered the house, the blind men came to him, and Jesus said to them, "Do you believe that I am able to do this?" They said to him, "Yes, Lord." [29]Then he touched their eyes, saying, "According to your faith be it done to you." [30]And their eyes were opened. And Jesus sternly warned them, "See that no one knows about it." [31]But they went away and spread his fame through all that district. [32]As they were going away, behold, a demon-oppressed man who was mute was brought to him. [33]And when the demon had been cast out, the mute man spoke. And the crowds marvelled, saying, "Never was anything like this seen in Israel." [34]But the Pharisees said, "He casts out demons by the prince of demons."

In his novel *Charlotte Gray*, Sebastian Faulks captures the sense of futility and meaninglessness that is the inevitable product of an atheistic view of our world. The philosophy with which he deals is expounded by the character Professor Levade in his speech at the mid-point of the novel:

Man is alone in the world... when he dies, there may be regrets among those left behind that they never knew him better, but he is forgotten almost as soon as he dies because there is no time for others to puzzle out his life. After a few years he will be referred to once or twice by a grandchild, then by no one at all. Unknown at the moment of birth, unknown after death. This weight of solitude! A being unknown.

It is almost as if this dismal conclusion is too much for Levade and so he continues:

> And yet, if I believe in God, I am known .... God will know me even as I cannot know myself ... I have for my companion the creator of the world. At the hour of my death I would wish to be "known unto God."

The rest of Faulks' novel explores the philosophy expounded by Levade through the fortunes of two sets of characters. Two small Jewish boys form one part of the plot. Their eventual fate is the gas chamber, and as their journey to extermination reaches its conclusion Faulks describes their end:

> There was another room, another door, with bolts and rubber seals, over whose threshold the two boys, among many others, went through icy air, and disappeared.

The other character is Charlotte Gray. Her 'end' is altogether different, and yet it is portrayed using almost identical language and imagery. She marries her lover and their wedding forms the closing scene of the novel, but Faulks describes her entry into the church by deliberately using the same phrases as he does for the boys crossing the entry into the gas chamber:

> She held tight onto his arm ... they crossed into the cold interior of the church, heavy with the scent of flowers and the murmuring of the organ, into the soft air, and disappeared.

The point of the novel is made with magnificent power and is hard to miss: whether we end our life prematurely in a gas chamber or end it in old age after years happily married to our beloved, without God, we are 'alone in this world ... unknown at the moment of birth, unknown after death. A being unknown'. Ultimately our existence, whether marked by heroism, joy and relational fulfilment or by wickedness, grief and extermination, is meaningless.

The point made so graphically by Faulks is one that has been noted by countless philosophers through the ages. Francis Bacon put it like this:

Man now realises that he is an accident. He is a completely futile being and has to play out the game without reason.[1]

Jean-Paul Sartre said:

Man is absurd. But he must grimly act as if he were not.[2]

The famous French scientist Jacques Monod concluded:

Man must at last wake ... to his total solitude, his fundamental isolation. Now does he at last realise that, like a gypsy, he lives on the boundary of an alien world? A world that is deaf to his music, just as indifferent to his hopes as it is to his suffering or his crimes ... Man knows at last that he is alone in the universe's unfeeling immensity, out of which he emerged only by chance. His destiny is nowhere spelled out, nor is his duty.[3]

Eventually any culture, society or individual that rejects God, whether it does so in the guise of fascism, communism or our own

---

[1] From an interview with Francis Bacon by David Sylvester in 1963, a transcript of which can be found in *Great Interviews of the 20th Century* published by *The Guardian*

[2] Jean-Paul Sartre, *Being and Nothingness*

[3] Jacques Monod *Chance and Necessity*, p 172, published by Penguin 1997

secularist liberal humanism, has to come to terms with the logical conclusion of its atheistic position. Without God there is no eternal purpose to life; we are ultimately unaccountable to any power or authority above and beyond the human race; we are alone. The fruits that flow from these philosophies can be read about in the history books and in the newspapers. Moral and societal disintegration is the inevitable product of the conclusion that there is no higher authority than the most powerful human force.

Against the sinister backcloth of these world-views, the truth of the Christian faith stands out like the most dazzling diamond. Our end is not simply to 'cross the threshold and disappear'; we are not 'alone in the universe's unfeeling immensity'; we are 'known unto God' and therefore there is point, purpose, direction and moral meaning to our lives.

With Jesus' arrival as King, God was revealing in the most dramatic way possible that mankind is not alone in this universe. Our passage begins in verses 14-17 as Jesus speaks of himself using the title '*Bridegroom*', evoking an important Old Testament image of God's kingdom.[4] Jesus is the long-awaited King, and the disciples' joy at his arrival is entirely appropriate. By using the pictures of '*new wine put into old wineskins*'(verse 17), and '*unshrunk cloth*' put on '*an old garment*' (verse 16), Jesus also implies that a radically new age is beginning. In talking about the Bridegroom being '*taken away*' he once again anticipates his own death and, as in chapter 8 verse 17, hints at the way in which this new era is to be established.

In verses 18-34 Matthew builds on this idea of the arrival of a new era by drawing together many of the themes that have been running since the start of chapter 8. (Preacher's Note 1) We are introduced to a ruler whose daughter has just died and to a

---

[4] The kingdom of God is frequently portrayed in the Old Testament as a marriage between God and Israel, with God or his king as the bridegroom and Israel as the bride (Isaiah 54, Psalm 45, Song of Songs).

woman whose incurable condition has left her isolated and alone in her suffering. These two characters provide a snapshot of the hopeless, helpless condition of humanity apart from the loving intervention of a creator God. In his dealing with the ruler and the woman with bleeding, Jesus confirms for us that God has a purpose for his creation and for his people beyond this age. This purpose is centred on Jesus, his King, and on the people whom Jesus calls to himself. God's people are 'known unto God' and in Jesus they 'have as their companion the creator of the world'. In Jesus there is hope and life beyond the grave.

The healing of the blind men in verses 27-31 shows us that it is by faith that a person is included in this kingdom, whilst the response to the casting out of the demon in verses 32-34 gives the first indication in Matthew's gospel of the deep division that Jesus will bring about between those who obey his command to follow and those who disobey.

Our world is not drifting meaninglessly through time and space. You and I are not 'absurd' or 'fundamentally isolated'. God exists and has a purpose for his people both within and beyond this universe. The king has arrived with all God's authority to establish his heavenly kingdom and to bring the blessing that his law anticipated. Matthew's aim in this section is that we respond in faith to what God is doing in Jesus and so step out from an existence of isolated futility that is the product of rejecting our creator.

Resurrection Life

Having introduced the theme of Jesus as Bridegroom bringing in the new age, Matthew goes on to narrate probably the most poignant scene in all Jesus' ministry. We have already noted that human death is the inevitable consequence of the Fall. [5] The death

---

[5] See the section on Sin, God's judgment and the shadow of death in chapter 1.

of a young girl (we read in Mark's gospel that she was only twelve) adds to grief a sense of futility and wasted possibility. In telling the story, Matthew makes it plain that the girl was quite definitely dead:

> Behold, a ruler came in and knelt before him, saying, "My daughter has just died, but come and lay your hand on her, and she will live." (verse 18)

With his customary brevity, it seems that Matthew has omitted the ruler's initial approach whilst the girl was still living, which is recorded by Mark in chapter 5 of his gospel (verses 22-24). The presence of official mourners in verses 23-25 of Matthew's account indicates that the funeral proceedings had started, and so we can be sure that the girl was not simply in a coma; she really was dead. Furthermore, their response to Jesus' comment that he was going to resurrect her is yet another indication that she was dead. The mourners' laughter shows that they thought the local healer had stepped way beyond his powers on this occasion. When Jesus said, *'Go away, for the girl is not dead but sleeping,'* that does not mean that he believed she was simply unconscious. Rather, to Jesus, with all his power and authority, raising a person from death was like waking a person up from sleep. Indeed, those with teenage daughters might note that Jesus performed his task with considerably greater ease! The eventual resurrection of the ruler's daughter by Jesus is evidence of the radically new era that Jesus had come to usher in. He is God's King with all God's absolute authority over death.

One of the most wretched parts of my job as a Church of England minister is that from time to time I have to preside at the funeral of a child. There can be no more dreadful example of the desperate consequences of life in a fallen world than the death of a little one. Whether it is in images of starving children on our screens or in our own personal experience, the grief, hopelessness and helpless impotence that one feels at the death of a child makes the ruler's approach to Jesus in verse 18 totally understandable. In Mark's gospel, we sense the father's agonised desperation as we read that he came and *'fell at his feet and implored him'*. Here Matthew uses different language to Mark and takes the word that he used to describe the worship of the Magi back in chapter 2 verses 2 and 11. Like the Eastern Kings before him, this ruler came into the house and *knelt* and spoke. Matthew loves to use this word and he does so to underline the identity of Jesus. He is the one with all God's absolute authority even over our greatest enemy, death itself. Humble obeisance is the only appropriate response to the majesty of Jesus, who has come to usher in a new era where death will be defeated once and for all. We are not, as Francis Bacon put it, 'completely futile beings' who have to 'play out the game without reason'.

Like the centurion in chapter 8, the ruler's logic was as flawless as his faith was absolute. He had identified Jesus for who he is and so he said:

"but come and lay your hand on her, and she will live."

However, before this incident came to its conclusion, there was an interruption.

As we turn to examine the woman with bleeding, we need to be asking ourselves why it is that Matthew chose to interrupt the action of the narrative and include this additional healing in his account. There can be no doubt that the woman's condition was as personally distressing as the ruler's grief was pitiful. She had *'suffered from a discharge of blood for twelve years.'* Her haemorrhaging menstrual disorder rendered her, and anything she touched, ceremonially unclean, for the law of the Old Testament declared:

if a woman has a discharge of blood for many days, ... she shall continue in uncleanness. (Leviticus 15 verse 25).

Strictly speaking, this woman ought not to have been mingling in the crowd; she certainly was forbidden from touching Jesus or anything that he was wearing. Indeed, her contact with his garment ought to have rendered Jesus himself ceremonially unclean. Instead, as with the leper and Peter's mother-in-law, Jesus spoke and the woman was made well.

All of this is relatively obvious from a first reading of this incident. However, it doesn't help us to work out why it is that Matthew has included the woman's healing alongside the resurrection of the ruler's daughter and the saying about the Bridegroom. After all, Jesus did many miracles, so many that *were every one of them to be written … the world itself could not contain the books that would be written.'* (John 21 verse 25). We know that Matthew includes only the barest essentials of most incidents that he records, and those that are included are carefully selected in order to make his key points. With this in mind, we have to ask ourselves why it is that Matthew chooses to include this healing. What is it that he wants us to learn?

I wonder if the key might be in the last words of verse 20. It seems to me that they contain a clue that ties in with the lesson Jesus taught from the parable of the new wine and new wineskins, and with the healing of the leper right back at the start of this narrative section in chapter 8 verses 1-4. We read in verse 20 that this woman *'touched the fringe of his garment.'* The *'fringe'* is actually the word for *'tassel'*, an important symbolic part of any Jew's clothing. [6] The tassel was worn as a reminder of everything that the law says, and by wearing it a Jewish person was showing his commitment to keep all of the law. You can find the details in Numbers 15 verses 37-41:

> And it shall be a tassel for you to look at and remember all the commandments of the Lord, to do them, not to follow after your own heart.

---

[6] Matthew uses the word with the same meaning in chapter 23 verse 5.

Now, as this woman comes to Jesus, Matthew notes that she touches the very part of his garment that was designed to remind her, and indeed all of us, of the law that had brought her condemnation.

It is almost impossible to imagine the suffering that this woman had undergone. She had been afflicted with this condition for twelve years. That would mean twelve years of deeply personal and intrusive medical treatment. All of it had failed. The law had been unable to help her, declaring her ceremonially unclean and demanding that she be symbolically excluded from God's presence and from all of the blessings that flowed from acceptance by him amongst his people. Rather than aiding her, the law had simply pronounced condemnation. As she came to God's long-awaited rescuing King, she found, in place of the exclusion and condemnation pronounced by the law, acceptance and inclusion. Once again this incident confirms for us the radically new era that Jesus, with all his authority as God's King, has come to establish.

On what basis is she healed? Jesus says:

"Take heart, daughter; your faith has made you well."

I love it that he calls her '*daughter*'. It may be that this was simply a regular term of address. However, in the context of the ruler and his dead daughter, we find Jesus addressing this woman as '*daughter*' and rescuing her from the isolation of spiritual and physical condemnation, enabling her to be welcomed back amongst God's people as a full member of God's family and included in all the blessings that come from belonging to the living God. In performing this healing miracle, Jesus, the long-awaited rescuing King, accomplished everything that the law anticipated but was unable to achieve without its fulfilment in Christ. This woman was 'known unto God'.

Meanwhile, it is hard to imagine what must have been going through the ruler's mind as Jesus delayed. Certainly the interruption serves to increase our certainty that the girl really was dead. As Jesus arrived at the ruler's house, the impression of a man acting with absolute divine authority is inescapable. He cut through the protests of the official mourning party, for he knew he was about to pronounce their redundancy: a new era had arrived. Before he even saw the girl, he declared his diagnosis:

"Go away, for the girl is not dead but sleeping."

The point is *not* that she was simply in a coma, but rather that to Jesus, who is the author of life and who has all of God's authority over life and death, death is not the end. Nor is this incident purely a demonstration of Jesus' raw authority. Its purpose at the end of the narrative of chapters 8 and 9 is to show us that Jesus has all authority as God's divine King to establish the long-promised kingdom where he reigns eternally and where death is defeated forever. He really had come to do the radically new thing that God promised his King would do [7].

We need to realise that this idea of the temporary nature of death is not introduced for the first time in the New Testament. The whole bible speaks of a final day when God will raise all people to judgment and give to his people eternal life in his land of blessing, whilst confining his enemies to eternal punishment (Daniel 12; Isaiah 25). This day is known as 'The Resurrection from the Dead'[8]. When Jesus confronted the Sadducees later in the gospel, he berated them for not believing in The Resurrection. He told them that they didn't believe it because they had failed either to grasp the power of God or to understand their bibles properly. (Preacher's Note 2) This aspect of God's future purpose

---

[7] Isaiah 25:6-9

[8] I am using capitals for The Resurrection of the Dead to make it clear that this refers to a particular day, such as Boxing Day or Thanksgiving Day

is developed through the rest of the Old Testament under the theme of God's kingdom and around the role of God's King.

This makes the titles that are given to Jesus through chapters 8 and 9 all the more significant. Jesus had just declared himself to be *the Bridegroom*. He had also either called himself, or been called, *Lord, Son of God,* and *Son of Man*, all of them Old Testament titles for the Messiah. God's long-awaited King was expected to come as the one who would rule everlastingly over an eternal kingdom. Passages that teach this from the Old Testament include the famous Isaiah chapter 9 that we read at carol services at Christmas. In this chapter, God promises a son who is nothing less than God himself and whose kingdom will endure forever. Similar ideas are to be found in 2 Samuel 7, Psalm 2 and Daniel 7, to name just a handful of the numerous promises of the Old Testament that look forward to the everlasting rule of the eternal Saviour King. This everlasting rule of God's eternal saviour will begin when he raises all the dead from every age, judges them, and establishes his New Creation at the same time as he confines his enemies to just judgment for eternity.

Given the repeated emphasis on Jesus as the long-awaited King in chapters 8 and 9, there is only one conclusion that we can rightly draw from Jesus' statement that the ruler's daughter is '*not dead but sleeping*', and from her subsequent resurrection: Jesus, as King, has come with all God's authority to establish his eternal kingdom. He is the one who will summon the dead from their graves on the last day. Peter and John were spot on in their preaching in Jerusalem when they were *proclaiming in Jesus The Resurrection of the Dead* (Acts 4 verse 2). Of course, we need to remember that he came *early*, as seen in chapter 8, but the point of this section is clear. One day our greatest enemy will be defeated. Everything that wrecks and spoils all our hopes and dreams in this world will be done away with forever. The King of kings has come, and with his authority as Lord of all lords he has absolute power to summon the dead from their sleep. His rule will accomplish everything that the law pointed to, and as we turn to follow him we shall find that we too are invited to enjoy the rich blessings of his kingdom rule even as he judges and overthrows all his enemies.

This means that the conclusion of the atheist is flawed. We are not, as Francis Bacon thought, 'an accident', nor are we 'completely futile beings'. Jesus has demonstrated that he is God and that he will achieve what God promised his King would accomplish.

I vividly remember the first funeral that I ever attended. My grandmother had died in her eighties, and our entire family was gathered at a small church in north Norfolk. The rain was driving almost horizontally as we stood around the grave and watched the coffin lowered. As I drove away from the scene, I was overwhelmed by a sense of the total pointlessness of life. We are a close family and our relationships are good. My grandmother's death seemed to make everything that we lived and worked for appear utterly futile. However, as I drove on, I began to preach the gospel of Jesus' kingdom to myself. My grandmother was a Christian, she knew Jesus Christ, and therefore she was not 'alone at the point of death'. The lowering of her body into the grave was by no means the end, indeed one might say it was merely the beginning! She was 'known unto God' and her soul was already with him in paradise. Indeed, one day her body will be raised by Jesus, the King of kings, the son of David, as he returns to summon her and all his people to his eternal kingdom.

It may well be that some readers of this book will have experienced the death of a child. As a parent stands at the grave of one of their children, it is possible for overwhelming grief to be mingled with a sense of futility, meaningless and wasted potential. These verses give deep and real assurance that death is not the end, that believers will one day be reunited with all God's people, that our existence is not like that of a 'gypsy on the boundary of an alien world', as Jacques Monod thought. Rather our creator God calls us to step out of an isolated, pointless existence in this world and into an eternal living relationship with him through his Son, the Lord Jesus Christ.

Credible Faith

All the way through the narrative of this second major section of Matthew's Gospel we have seen an emphasis on the faith that is necessary in order to benefit from the arrival of the King. The centurion is commended for his unique faith (chapter 8 verse 10); the disciples are rebuked for their miniscule faith (chapter 8 verse 26); the friends of the paralytic are rewarded for their active faith (chapter 9 verse 2); the woman with bleeding is encouraged on account of her courageous faith (chapter 9 verse 22). Clearly, faith is required for membership of Jesus' heavenly kingdom.

In the penultimate incident of this section, the theme of faith receives close attention. As in the incident with the leper at the beginning of chapter 8, the presence of two blind men in God's promised land, where God's blessings were meant to be experienced in abundance, is evidence that all was not well in Israel. Their healing demonstrates that God's promise in Isaiah 35 verse 5 that *'the eyes of the blind shall be opened'* was being fulfilled, undeniable proof that Jesus had come as Messiah to establish God's long-promised kingdom of heaven.

However, the focus of verses 27-31 is as much on the nature of the faith of these two men as it is on their healing. In their persistent request for help and in the subsequent interview with Jesus, the theme of genuine biblical faith, which has been such a big part of this section, reaches its conclusion. By placing these verses here, Matthew focuses attention on the kind of response that is expected from those who are to be 'known unto God' and who will become part of the kingdom of heaven. There are at least three points to note.

Firstly, saving faith involves a subjective response to an objective fact. The two blind men gave Jesus possibly the most exalted Messianic title in the whole of this narrative section. The term *'son of David'* identifies Jesus plainly as the long-awaited King. Matthew uses this term frequently, starting with the opening verse of his gospel:

> The book of the genealogy of Jesus Christ, the son of David,
> the son of Abraham. (Matthew chapter 1 verse 1)

The use of this Messianic title shows us that the faith of these two men was not a blind leap in the dark. Though they could not see physically, they had twenty-twenty perception when it came to Jesus' identity, and they concluded that he was *the son of David*. Thus their request was not wishful thinking; it was grounded in facts that had been observed and weighed, and their action was driven by logical conclusions.

This is immensely important for us to grasp, since there is so much misunderstanding about the nature of Christian faith. I have lost count of the number of times people have said to me, 'I wish I had *your* faith', as if faith were something magical that is conjured up within a person, with no objective logical basis. In chapters 8 and 9 of his gospel, Matthew is at pains to lay out for us the clear evidence for who Jesus is and what he had come to do. The blind men had clearly 'seen' this. They had weighed the facts and come to a proper conclusion that Jesus is *the son of David*, and so they came to him for help. This is true biblical faith; as the Apostle Paul says, *faith comes from hearing* (Romans 10 verse 17). True faith comes as a result of careful examination of the facts of history.

Lewis Carroll manages to capture the popular misunderstanding of faith in his book, *Through the Looking Glass*. The White Queen asks Alice to believe that she is 'just one hundred and one, five months and a day.' When Alice protests at being asked to believe something so ridiculous, the Queen replies: 'try again, take a long breath, and shut your eyes.' Alice is not persuaded; 'one *can't* believe impossible things,' she says. To which the Queen replies: 'I dare say you haven't had much practice … When I was your age, I always did it for half an hour a day. Why, sometimes I've believed as many as six impossible things before breakfast.'

True biblical faith is not a matter of immature children 'believing six unbelievable things before breakfast'. True biblical faith comes as we look closely at the evidence and take appropriate action; it is a subjective response to objective reality.

Secondly, true saving faith comes through divine revelation, not through human reason. This is not to contradict the point that we have just been exploring, for the things God shows us in his revelation are logical, reasonable and objectively true. However, we need to recognise that genuine biblical faith is a gift from God and does not come through our capacity to work things out. After all, if it were the case that we could reason our way to God, the God we believe in would only be as big as our reason. This point is made through these two blind men, who exemplify God's promise through Isaiah that his King would come to give sight to the blind. Blindness in Isaiah is used as a picture to describe the spiritual state of Israel. When God promises to give sight to the blind in Isaiah 35, he is not intending that we all head off to set up eye-hospitals (though this is a fine thing for Christians to do). The point of declaring that the blind will receive sight is that God himself was going to break in and give spiritual sight to the spiritually blind who had rejected God's rule. These two blind men symbolised the spiritual state of Israel: they could not see. By touching their eyes and giving them sight, Jesus provided a graphic physical symbol of the internal spiritual work that had taken place in their lives as they were enabled to see Jesus for who he truly is and for what he had come to do.

In one sense, the person who says to us, 'I wish I had your faith', is right. Faith is a gift, and spiritual sight comes only as God enables a person to see. When someone says something like that to me, I always reply, 'why don't you ask God for it?' However, I follow up that reply with an encouragement to start examining the life and work of Jesus because, as we saw earlier, *'faith comes from hearing'*.

The final thing to notice about these men's faith is that it is persistent and that it is public. They followed Jesus *'crying aloud'*. This was no 'flash-in-the-pan' affair. They had seen who Jesus is and they were determined to meet him and have him help them. Furthermore, as Jesus interviewed them, they confessed with their lips, and then once he had healed them, they *'went away and spread his fame through all that district'*. They simply couldn't keep their mouths shut! The Apostle Paul tells us, *'with the heart one believes and is justified, and with the mouth one confesses and is saved'* (Romans 10 verse 10). The brief interview with Jesus in chapter 9 verse 28 is interesting, for it seems that Jesus was determined to get them to state publicly what was blindingly obvious! He asked, *'Do you believe that I am able to do this?'* Given that they had been following him, crying out for him to save them, his question seems almost redundant. Nonetheless, he still asked them to speak about what they wanted from him and why. I am sure that this is intended to show us that they confessed their faith openly. This theme of public profession was further emphasised by their actions in verse 31. It appears that they went straight out and wilfully disobeyed Jesus, for he had just *'sternly warned them,"see that no one knows about it"'*, yet there is no comment either from Jesus or from Matthew about the rights or wrongs of their action. Possibly this is in order to indicate to us that it will never be possible to hide genuine faith. This ties in with one of the major thrusts of chapter 10, which will be explored in subsequent chapters of the book.

Known to God

As Matthew draws his narrative to its conclusion, he wants us to see what is required if we are to benefit from the kingdom that Jesus has come to establish. Membership of God's kingdom comes through faith. True faith is a gift from God. True faith is a reasonable response to the truth that God has shown us in Jesus. True faith will never remain a purely private affair. These three aspects of genuine faith are at the same time both humbling and challenging. No Christian person can ever afford to allow feelings of superiority or self-satisfaction to creep into their discipleship.

All of us were at one time spiritually blind. It is only the work of God breaking into our lives and giving us sight that has enabled us see Jesus for who he is and to put our trust in him. At the same time, no Christian person can ever afford to grow complacent in the desire for a deeper understanding and grasp of Jesus. True faith is founded in the person of Jesus, so as we grow to know him better, our faith will be stronger. This sort of faith, given to us by Jesus, unites us to God and ties us into his eternal purposes, flooding our lives with meaning and direction as they are refocused for his glory.

We began this chapter with a brief examination of the futility of the atheist's view of the world. Without God, man is 'alone in this world' ... 'unknown at the moment of birth, unknown after death. This weight of solitude, a being unknown.' The first two characters in the narrative bring the issues of futility and isolation into sharp focus. The woman was alone, cut off and shunned; the ruler, facing the death of his daughter, had come face to face with the pointlessness of existence in a most brutal way. In the raising of the dead child and the healing of the woman, Jesus demonstrated graphically that the atheist is wrong. Only God can do the things Jesus did here, so in doing them Jesus showed that God has broken into this fallen world and offers a radical alternative to all who trust in him. Some would argue that turning to trust Jesus is on a par with believing in fairies at the bottom of the garden. This is Richard Dawkins' point in his book *The God Delusion*. However, genuine biblical faith is an altogether logical response to the facts of history seen in the life and work of Jesus Christ. As a person puts their trust in Jesus, they are brought out of isolated futility into a living relationship with the one who will, one day, summon all from their graves to judgment and who will give to his people a place in his perfect New Creation.

Divisive Authority

The final incident in the narrative (verses 32-34), the healing of the dumb man, was yet another public example of the authority of Jesus, illustrating another of the promises found in Isaiah's prophecy:

> the ears of the deaf [shall be] unstopped (Isaiah 35 verse 5).

This healing brings to the surface something that will be a major emphasis both in the discourse of chapter 10 and in the next major section of the gospel that runs from chapter 11 to chapter 13. The key verse of that section is chapter 11 verse 12:

> "From the days of John the Baptist until now, the kingdom of heaven has been forcefully advancing, and forceful men lay hold of it" (NIV).

This verse explains that division is inevitable even as Jesus' kingdom advances unstoppably.

The crowd's response to Jesus' authority as he cast out the demon was one of only two possible interpretations. They '*marvelled*', for they realised that the supernatural nature of the healing of the dumb man meant that something greater than human authority was at work. Jesus must have been working with the divine authority of God. The Pharisees, of course, could not accept this, and suggested something more sinister was happening, an argument they return to, and Jesus refutes, in chapter 11.

Suggested questions for group or personal study

1. If there is no God and death is the end of life, what implications are there for the purpose of life and the moral decisions we take on earth?

2.   How does Matthew's description of the ruler's approach to Jesus serve to express both the emotion of the moment and the extent of the ruler's faith?

3.   How does Matthew indicate that the girl is definitely dead? Jesus says that she was *'sleeping'*. What does this suggest about Jesus' view of death?

4.   The raising of the ruler's daughter is interrupted by the woman with bleeding. Look up Leviticus chapter 15 verse 25. How does this verse help us to understand the woman's condition?

5.   The woman was healed by touching the tassel on Jesus' garment. Numbers 25 verses 37-41 tells us that the purpose of this tassel was to remind people of the law of Moses. What did the law demand of the woman? How does this incident serve to show us that Jesus achieves what the law anticipated? How does this relate to Matthew chapter 9 verses 14-17?

6.   Jesus does raise the ruler's daughter. How does this serve to confirm Jesus' identity for us? What are the implications for the purpose of life? How would these verses serve to help a person experiencing grief?

7.   What lessons can we learn about genuine faith from verses 27-31?

8.   What is required if we are to benefit from the kingdom of Jesus? How do these verses humble and challenge us when it comes to our faith?

9.   Verses 32-34 give us an indication of the kinds of response that we should expect to the kingdom of Jesus. Why do people respond in these ways?

Preacher's Note 1

Many treat Jesus' statement about new wine and new wineskins as if the primary purpose of the teaching is to indicate that new structures are needed to accommodate the work that Jesus has come to do. Certainly this point is valid and is supported by the calling of the Apostles just a few verses later. However, this exposition takes the line that simply to speak in terms of new structures risks underplaying what is going on in the rest of these chapters. The use of Bridegroom in these verses is a Messianic concept and is therefore designed to draw on the rest of the Messianic material in chapters 8 and 9. The point Matthew is alerting us to is that Jesus' coming is an eschatological breaking in, ahead of time, of the Royal King. Certainly this will require new structures, but to limit our exposition simply to the new structures is to miss the big point that he has arrived to usher in the new era that will culminate in him establishing the New Creation at the Resurrection from the Dead. The raising of the ruler's daughter points us forward to the final Resurrection of the Dead and confirms that Jesus is the Royal Bridegroom who has come to do what the Law anticipated.

Preacher's Note 2

The implication of the passage in Matthew 22 verses 23-32 is that Abraham, Isaac and Jacob all believed in the great day of The Resurrection, when the dead will be summoned to judgment and God will establish his eternal rule. This means that those who suggest that the Old Testament believers had no concept of Resurrection and of Eternal Life have also failed to read the Old Testament correctly. Jesus' implication is that the Old Testament teaches the Resurrection of the Dead, and that it does so on its own terms. When I was taught theology at a liberal theological college and in a liberal university faculty, it was suggested to me on more than one occasion that the Old Testament believer had little or no concept of resurrection from death. However, according to Jesus, if we fail to see this from our Old Testament studies then we have failed both to see the power of God and to understand his word.

FOUR

Understanding the Times of the Kingdom

Matthew 9:35-38

[35]And Jesus went throughout all the cities and villages, teaching in their synagogues and proclaiming the gospel of the kingdom and healing every disease and every affliction. [36]When he saw the crowds, he had compassion for them, because they were harassed and helpless, like sheep without a shepherd. [37]Then he said to his disciples, "The harvest is plentiful, but the labourers are few; [38]therefore pray earnestly to the Lord of the harvest to send out labourers into his harvest."

The Dorchester Gladiators is a small rugby football club of veteran players from the south coast of England. A few years ago, the Dorchester Gladiators went on tour to Romania. A slight error in translation meant that, instead of playing against a side of similarly decrepit 50 to 60-year-olds, they found themselves in Bucharest, in the national stadium, on national television, playing the Romanian national side. Nigel Jones, a relatively youthful 49-year-old, said:

> We started to get worried when our hosts asked us if we wanted to do a training session the night before. This is not exactly our style. So we did our pre-match build-up in the bar and didn't get to bed until 4 in the morning. When the morning came, they started warming up professionally; we just stood around smoking, knowing we were in real trouble.

The Dorchester Gladiators had misunderstood the terms of engagement, and therefore they ended up seriously embarrassed. It is all too easy for us to be like that as Christians. In order to be rightly orientated to the mission that God has given to us as the disciples of Jesus Christ, we need to understand the terms and conditions of what we're engaged in. If we don't, we will find ourselves disillusioned, disappointed and disorientated as we go about engaging in the work that he has given us to do.

We have already noted that Matthew's aim in the second section of his gospel is to demonstrate that Jesus, God's King, has arrived with all of God's authority as his saviour for our world; he wants us to understand the times. In the next three chapters we shall be studying the discourse, or teach-in, which follows the narrative of chapters 8 and 9. As Jesus expounds and applies what it means for his disciples to live in the light of his arrival, we shall find the times, the terms and conditions, and the family ties of the kingdom laid out for us. The aim of the discourse is to prevent us engaging in Christian discipleship without being clear on what it will entail.

Personally, I find Matthew's inclusion of this teaching wonderfully refreshing. There is no 'small print' when it comes to Jesus' call to discipleship. He makes it crystal clear upfront what it will cost to belong to him, even as he spells out the implications of refusing him and the positive incentives as to why we should take up our cross and follow.

As we study the discourse, we shall find that part of this section is specific only to the original band of twelve apostles, but the principles of the vast majority of it are applicable to every single disciple.

A time for clear-headed kingdom conviction

Verse 35 of chapter 9 provides a summary of the first major theme that we find running through the narrative of chapters 8 and 9:

> Jesus went throughout all the cities and villages, teaching in their synagogues and proclaiming the gospel of the kingdom and healing every disease and every affliction.

Matthew reminds us that there was a time in Galilee, as Jesus moved through the towns and villages, when all the visible, physical effects of human rebellion against God, which symbolised God's judgment on his people Israel, were reversed. (Preacher's Note 1) For a brief moment, it was as if heaven came to earth: the King had arrived! As a leper was cleansed, the shroud of death and God's judgment on humanity was rolled back; as a centurion's servant was healed, the nations were declared welcome at the heavenly banquet; as the sick of Capernaum came to Jesus and were made well, we saw this was possible because Jesus would die the sin-bearing, substitutional death of God's servant King. The matchless majesty of the Lord of creation was demonstrated as Jesus stilled the raging elements with a word; God's power to destroy evil was seen as Jesus released two men from the grip of demons; the Son of Man's authority on earth to forgive sins was proved as a paralysed man leapt from his bed with the body of a young athlete; and finally, Jesus' divine authority and glorious resurrection rule was seen as he raised a young girl from death, restoring her life. There was a period in Galilee in the first century when all the effects of living in a fallen world, the likes of which we see so dramatically played out on our screens and in our lives day after day, were reversed. It is as if the hospital wards of Galilee General Hospital were closed, the accident and emergency department was deserted, there was no sound of a siren, no waiting lists, no prescriptions, no physios, no medical insurance. The health service budget was reduced to nil. For a brief moment, heaven came to earth.

I love speaking on these verses in St Helen's at our Sunday evening and Tuesday lunchtime services. On a Sunday evening we have many medical students attending. I like to remind them that if they had been in Galilee in the first century, they would have been redundant! On a Tuesday lunchtime there are numerous men and women who work in the insurance sector. When the King of kings walked the earth, there was no need for underwriters or brokers, for the King of creation had arrived and the elements were in submission to him.

However, as we consider the arrival of the King, we do need to get our thinking clear in order to avoid becoming seriously disorientated. We need to consider in what sense Jesus had arrived as King of the kingdom. In order to be clear-headed, we need to go back to the very heart of the narrative section in chapter 8. The demons' words to Jesus in chapter 8 verse 29 demonstrate their understanding that there is a day when they will be totally destroyed by Jesus:

> "What have you to do with us, O Son of God? Have you come here to torment us before the time?"

The demons realised the truth of Psalm 2 and Psalm 110, that there is a time set when all the enemies of God's King will be utterly destroyed; the King of kings will make his enemies a footstool for his feet and dash them to pieces. However, the demons also recognised that the King of kings had come early, before the appointed time. This recognition by the demons that Jesus had not yet come to destroy all evil forever whilst he lived on earth in human flesh, enables us to understand the sense in which his kingdom has arrived. You will remember that, with the rigorous logic of the tax collector, Matthew records for us in chapter 9 verse 6 Jesus' explanation as to why he had come early:

"the Son of Man has authority on earth to forgive sins."

Jesus came in advance of his final destruction of all evil in order to forgive sin and to summon sinners to enjoy the glorious heavenly banquet that he has prepared for his people from every nation at the end of time.

So then, though he will come one day to destroy all the forces of evil, to judge those who have rebelled against God and to banish them, he has not come to do that *yet*. His first coming provides us with just a foretaste of what his new creation will be like and gives us clear reasons as to why we should want to follow him. It does not, however, provide us with a picture of what life is meant to be like as we follow him today.

Those of us who are familiar with the vagaries of the English weather will know that there is sometimes a brief spell lasting a few days in the middle or at end of March when, after months of rain, frost, gloomy cloudiness and occasional snow, the sun comes out. The gloom of November and December, January and February lifts, the daffodils start to emerge, the birds begin to sing, the evenings aren't quite so long, and we begin to realise that yes, there is hope! Spring could be just around the corner. There's a place on the farm where I grew up where you can sit in the shelter outdoors even in the middle of February and March and feel warm! Almost invariably, however, after just a few days, the skies close in again, the rain starts to fall and we have to face the fact that summer has not arrived yet. As Jesus walked the earth, he gave us one of those sky-clearing moments, a brief glimpse of his long-promised kingdom. While he walked the earth in Galilee for a three-year period, we were given a glimpse of what his heavenly kingdom is going to be like. C S Lewis captures something of this foretaste of heaven in his children's story, *The Lion the Witch and the Wardrobe*, and it is depicted beautifully in the first of the Narnia films when, near the beginning, the lion Aslan (who represents Jesus) passes through the Ice Queen's kingdom. The snow begins to melt, the trees start to bud – but then Aslan moves away, and the Ice Queen's kingdom freezes over again.

If we are to have clear-headed conviction, we need to realise that Jesus' first coming was a coming 'ahead of time', with the specific purpose of summoning and saving sinners for his kingdom. It is only at his second coming and at The Resurrection of the Dead that he will destroy evil absolutely as his New Creation rule begins.

This means that the painful reality of living in a fallen world will still be very much the norm for true Christian disciples. The time has not yet come when we can wake up to a world free from the atrocities of Darfur or the horrors of tsunamis and typhoons, nor is it the time yet for all sickness and disease to be banished. Instead this is the time for forgiveness of sins and the summoning of sinners from across the world to be part of the future glory of Jesus' heavenly banquet.

Many of us will have come across the kind of Christian teaching that suggests that it is God's desire for all true Christians to enjoy health and wealth in abundance in this life. For obvious reasons, this teaching is known as the 'prosperity gospel'. It is immensely dangerous, for by running completely counter to what we are taught by Jesus and his apostles in the New Testament, it encourages totally inappropriate expectations of what it means to follow Jesus today. The result is that those who accept the so-called 'prosperity gospel' end up disillusioned with Jesus and doubtful of his claims, simply because they have been given a muddle-headed understanding of the times in which we live. Once we gain a clear-headed understanding of the times, the truth of chapter 9 verse 35 – that Jesus has arrived as God's long-awaited King with all God's authority to rescue his people – serves to strengthen and fortify genuine Christian discipleship.

Personally, I have found this point enormously helpful for my own perseverance in Christian ministry. I remember as a young Christian wondering what on earth was the matter with the 40 and 50 year olds in the church. Not only did many of them appear to have physical middle-age spread, they seemed also to have the spiritual equivalent. As I have grown older as a Christian, I have begun to see some of the struggles and obstacles to remaining keenly zealous in Christian discipleship. Contrary to the expectations of the young convert, it does not grow any easier to stay fervent as age advances. Indeed, I sometimes compare myself to one of the early personal computers, where one pushed the 'on' button and then waited for what seemed like an eternity before there was a flicker of life! The same can be true spiritually. As we grow older, it can be the case that we grow weary or find some of the original passion in discipleship wearing off. There may have been disappointments, worries and increased pressures; we may have faced setbacks and body blows to our faith, and the enemy may appear more real than ever. I find that to be the case particularly after a period of very active ministry, or indeed on returning from a really good holiday. The truths of these chapters have been enormously helpful to me at times like that. They are in effect the truths of the gospel, and I find that as I preach them to myself, flickers of life appear as God uses them to energise and inspire me for further action by his Spirit.

In times of spiritual lethargy, I will sometimes pose myself the questions: 'Has anything changed?' 'Has something happened that means we are no longer living in a time when Jesus is enthroned as Lord?' 'Is there some new revelation, something that God has done or said to tell us that times have changed?' As I go through the questions, the answer to each is a resounding: 'No!' The unchanging truths of the gospel are unchanged! So I ask myself one further question: 'It is still the time for proclaiming the forgiveness of sins and for summoning sinners to follow Jesus?' The answer is a resounding: 'Yes!' So then I say to myself: 'Stop moping about the place; understand the times, get ready to proclaim the gospel in the power of the Spirit and with the eagerness of someone who knows the days in which we live.' Preaching the gospel to yourself is a powerful antidote to spiritual lethargy!

A time for gut-wrenching kingdom compassion

Verse 36 of chapter 9 summarises the second major theme that we find running through chapters 8 and 9:

> When he [Jesus] saw the crowds, he had compassion for them, because they were harassed and helpless, like sheep without a shepherd.

Jesus responded to the crowds who were living under, and experiencing, the effects of man's rebellion against God not with what we might call finger-wagging, moral high-horsemanship. Instead, he responded with gut-wrenching compassion. There is a tabloid newspaper in the United Kingdom which has a particular reputation for censorious condemnatory attitudes. As you read it, you can guarantee that on many moral issues there will be the response of middle-class, finger-wagging, moral high-horsemanship. I like to suggest that it is just the newspaper for grumpy old men!

As Jesus looked out on the crowds, there was no hint of the tabloid editorial. Instead, when he saw the crowds, he had 'compassion'. I use the phrase 'gut-wrenching compassion' because the Greek word translated 'compassion' comes from a root meaning 'entrails' or 'innards'. It conveys the sense of how we feel something deep down in our stomach.

As Jesus looked out on the crowd, he saw them in a state of defenceless confusion, like a flock of sheep. The word 'sheep' is used regularly in the bible for God's people. We find it in Psalm 23: 'The Lord is my shepherd; I shall not want.' Psalm 100 describes us as 'the *sheep of his pasture'*, and there are many other examples of its use. The word translated *'harassed'* has a Greek root meaning 'to skin' or 'to flay'. The word translated as *'helpless'* comes from a word meaning 'to cast or throw', so perhaps it would be more appropriate to translate it 'scattered'. So we could translate verse 36:

> When Jesus saw the crowds, he had a gut-wrenching feeling for them, because they were being ripped to shreds and scattered abroad like a flock of sheep with no-one to watch over and protect them.

The phrase *'sheep without a shepherd'* also has a history in the bible. It was used by Moses as he expressed his longing for somebody to lead and shepherd the flock after his departure (Numbers 26 verses 16–17). It was used by God to describe his people when the kings had failed utterly; he described them as *'scattered on the mountains, as sheep that have no shepherd* (1 Kings 22 verse 17). In Ezekiel 34 verse 16, God promised that he would overthrow the false shepherds of his sheep and that he, the Lord, would shepherd them:

> "I will seek the lost, and I will bring back the strayed, and I will bind up the injured, and I will strengthen the weak, and the fat and the strong I will destroy. I will feed them in justice."

He goes on in verse 23 to promise:

> "I will set up over them one shepherd, my servant David, and he shall feed them … I, the Lord, will be their God, and my servant David shall be prince among them."

Anyone who has ever seen an unprotected, shepherd-less flock will be able to confirm that domestic sheep have no defence weapons; they have no great turn of speed, they are remarkably stupid, and the only hope of the domestic sheep is that the shepherd will stand his ground to defend them against the predator. Jesus looked out on the vast crowds under the failed leadership of first century Israel, suffering under the reality of God's judgment and wrath, and he responded with the deep compassion of the true Shepherd, God's long-awaited Royal Ruler.

The crowds must have included the people at whom the moral high-horsemen of Jesus' day tutted and wagged their fingers. No doubt Matthew was there, and many of his cronies, the sinners whom he had invited to dine at his house. The crowds would have included many who, in just a matter of months, would be baying for Jesus' crucifixion. Yet, as the Lord looked out on the vast crowd, he had compassion.

Jesus' response as the true shepherd of God's sheep is yet another indication that he is God's long-awaited saviour king, to whom the prophecies of Ezekiel 34 pointed. At the same time, Jesus' response shows us the way that he expects his people to respond to the lost world in the times in which we live. If we understand the times, we will respond to these days of 'sheep without a shepherd' with gut-wrenching kingdom compassion.

Notice where Jesus does and where he does not apportion the blame in verse 36. It is at least implicitly directed at those who should have been shepherding the flock, the leaders of God's people, the failed leadership of Israel's establishment.

I remember, with all the arrogance of a young 25-year-old, saying to my father, 'what is it that your generation did to turn what seemed to be a God-fearing nation in England into the hopeless, godless state that we are now in?' My father is a great man and he responded with characteristic patience and remarkable insight. He looked at me and said, 'William, the problem over the last 50 years has not been with the people, it has been with the leadership of the church'. Where the leadership of God's people is inadequate or ungodly, the people become like sheep without a shepherd, defenceless against the wolves of the world, the flesh and the devil. The proper response to such a situation is not the high-handed condemnation of the Pharisee, but the heartfelt compassion of the Lord.

We have already noted that (like verse 35) verse 36 is a summary verse. As we look back over chapters 8 and 9, we can observe the people of Galilee experiencing all the effects of living under God's judgment. Over and again Jesus responded to all he found with gut-wrenching compassion, for he had come with all of God's authority to save his people and to summon sinners. This is just how he reacted to the leper, the centurion, Peter's mother-in-law, the people of Capernaeum, the disciples on the boat, the demoniacs, the paralytic, Matthew, the synagogue ruler and the woman with bleeding.

This attitude of Jesus, summarised in chapter 9 verse 36, presents us with a serious challenge. If this was Jesus' attitude to his fallen people Israel, then it is also God's attitude to the world for which he lovingly gave his only Son. It shows us how all true disciples ought to respond to those who are living in a fallen world. Now, as then, is the time for forgiveness, now is the time for mercy, now is the time to summon sinners to repent and turn back to the King of kings. Now is not primarily the time for finger-wagging, moral high-horsemanship, for the Good Shepherd has arrived to seek the lost and bring back the strayed, to bind up the injured and strengthen the weak, and to destroy the fat and false shepherds that terrorise the flocks of people in the United Kingdom and elsewhere.

As we look at the United Kingdom today, there can be no doubt that we live in a nation that is experiencing the effects of being in rebellion against God. Os Guiness has described the state of a nation where the spiritual leaders have jettisoned God's word as heading 'back to the moral Stone Age'.[1] As we look at the United Kingdom today, we have to say that this appears to be the direction in which we are going.

One of the things God tells us about a culture that rejects him, is that he will give people over to 'the lusts of their hearts'

---

[1] *Time for Truth* p. 21, Os Guiness, published by IVP

(Romans 1 verse 24ff). Recently I did some research on the sexually transmitted disease statistics. In the United Kingdom, since 1995, the increase in reported cases of gonorrhea has been 139%, of chlamydia 192%, and of syphilis 1008%. This is just a foretaste of God's judgment, a window on hell. How should Christian disciples respond to such figures? Of course, we should acknowledge publicly that sexual promiscuity is wrong and that the attempts by liberal humanists to impose a secularist agenda on our nation have proven to have disastrous consequences. It is now increasingly evident that life-long marriage between two people of the opposite sex is the only place for safe sex, and that traditional families are the essential building blocks of stable societies. However, alongside this proper condemnation of the folly of atheism, it is all too easy for Christians to develop an inner attitude of finger-wagging moral high-horsemanship. Just as Jesus went to Matthew's house and ate with *'tax collectors and sinners'*, so we Christians must resist the temptation to distance ourselves from our fallen society when we have been shown that the time is here for summoning sinners.

Another thing we are told in the bible about a culture that rejects the knowledge of God, is that God will give it up to lawlessness, drunkenness and debauched living. (See, for instance Romans 1 verses 28-31; 1 Timothy 1 verses 9-11; Galatians 5 verses 19-21). As we consider the current plague of violent crime on the streets of the major cities of the United Kingdom, we cannot but acknowledge the bible's diagnosis of our culture. Having given up on God, our culture is experiencing the consequences of that decision. In the run-up to Christmas last year, the whole of one evening news bulletin was devoted to showing the need for extra police and ambulances to meet the binge-drinking associated with the Christmas festivities. Cardiff's Millennium Stadium was transformed into an ambulance centre to deal with the Friday night problems. Once again, as we consider how Christians ought to respond, we are right to insist that Christians acknowledge publicly the sheer folly of a secularist agenda that seeks only to apply the sticking-plasters of education, social action and more legislation to the problem. These problems flow from the heart of a nation which has turned its back on God. We are also right to acknowledge that the binge-drinking and violent crime culture is profoundly wrong. However, at the same time, as Christians, we must be aware of the acute danger of becoming like the Pharisees of Matthew 9 verse 11, rather than like the compassionate Lord of Matthew chapter 9 verse 36.

Peter Cameron Scott was one of the first missionaries to East Africa, landing in Mombasa in 1895. A year later, one week before his death, Scott witnessed a group of men sacrificing a goat, the idolatry of which must have appalled him. This is what he wrote in his diary:

They have hazy ideas about God, but how far from the truth. Can we whose souls are lighted with wisdom from on high, can we to men benighted the lamp of life deny?[2]

Now that is the mark of somebody with gut-wrenching compassion, who understands the times in which we live. I wonder if we could write the same about sophisticated London? What hazy ideas of God people have, but how far from the truth they are! 'Can we whose souls are lighted with wisdom from on high, can we to men benighted the lamp of life deny?' It may well be that there is need for real repentance in our churches when it comes to this point of gut-wrenching compassion. Conservative evangelicals tend to have a great and good desire for godliness, but as we look out on the devastation that has been caused by our nation's rejection of God, our response can so often be to retreat into the ghetto, wagging our condemnatory finger at our culture, just as the Pharisees did

[2] quoted in *We Felt Like Grasshoppers: The Story of Africa Inland Mission*, Dick Anderson, published by Crossway Books, 1994

in chapter 9 at the party that rocked the religious. The truly godly response is that of the Good Shepherd, who came into the world as the Son of Man with all of God's '*authority on earth to forgive sins*' and to command sinners to '*follow me*'.

A time for earnest and urgent prayer

Having summarised the two major themes of the narrative of chapters 8 and 9, Jesus now calls his disciples to action.

> Then he said to his disciples, "The harvest is plentiful, but the labourers are few; therefore pray earnestly to the Lord of the harvest to send out labourers into his harvest."
> (verses 37-8)

It is vital that we include Jesus' exhortation to prayer in verses 37-8 in this study, because otherwise our compassion might become little more than a hand-wringing, helpless feeling. Jesus does not want our gut-wrenching compassion to result in passive inactivity. In these verses, he shows us the proper response of the disciple who has both a clear conviction about the times in which we live and a gut-wrenching compassion for the lost. Such a person should respond with earnest, urgent, sustained prayer.

The striking thing is what Jesus does *not* command us to do as our first step in compassionate response. If I had written verse 37, I think I would have said: 'Jesus looked out on the crowds with great compassion, and so he decided to start up a training scheme and develop a business plan and spread it across the world.' However, for those who feel disgust at the leadership of the liberal establishment, Jesus does not command that we initiate a political lobbying group, nor does he tell us to organise a march on Broadcasting House or even to set up a social workers' symposium. He doesn't even set up a theological college, a ministry training scheme or a tools-for-ministry course (though such things can be very helpful!). Instead, the true mark of Christ-like compassion is to pray.

It is also striking to notice what he does and what he does not command us to pray for. How might you or I have completed this sentence:

Then he said to his disciples, "The harvest is plentiful, but the labourers are few; therefore pray earnestly to the Lord of the harvest ..."

Most naturally, I think, I would have expected to be told to pray for revival, but Jesus does not tell us to pray for that here. Instead, Jesus assumes that there is no shortage of harvest at all, but that it is *harvesters* who are needed. There is a dearth of well-trained, committed, convinced and clear-thinking compassionate labourers. The word '*labourer*' here is the word for a manual worker, and the picture is of a man stripped to his waist, with sweat dripping from his body, as he engages in tough manual endeavour. We are not talking about the archetypal British labourer leaning on his shovel! So, says Jesus, there is no problem with the harvest, what is needed is labourers. Notice that Jesus is not speaking simply about full-time, paid ministry. He has in mind ordinary Christians, prepared and ready to roll up their sleeves and get involved in the work of the gospel.

Two years ago in England we experienced the kind of harvest that farmers dream about. In the orchard on the farm where my parents live, the trees were groaning with the weight of apples. I remember walking through them at the end of August, and observing that the boughs were bent right over, with much of the fruit growing in the grass. What is needed at a time like that? Labourers! In Matthew chapter 9 verse 37 Jesus tells us, '*The harvest is plentiful*' – there is much of it out there – '*but the labourers are few.*'

It is very easy for those of us in the West who are living with the harsh reality of a post-Christian culture to assume that there is no harvest anywhere. It may be the case that in our part of the world the harvest does appear to be limited. However, as we take a global perspective, that is certainly not the case. All over the world there is a shortage of well trained, committed and clear-thinking labourers. We should pray then for labourers to be sent out into the harvest fields of the world.

In summary, then, understanding the times means understanding that the true royal shepherd of God's flock has arrived, that he is enthroned, and that he is exalted as Lord of all. One day he will come again to usher in his New Creation, and to destroy all evil. Now, however, is a time for forgiveness of sins, and now is still the time to summon sinners. The time has come, therefore, for a labour force which understands the times and has a clear-headed conviction and a gut-wrenching compassion, ready to be 'sent out' by God. The word translated *'sent out'* means literally *'thrust out'* – two words are combined in the original language, 'out' and 'to throw'. As we give ourselves to prayer of this sort, the implication is that God himself will do the work of thrusting labourers into his harvest field. Our job is to engage in earnest, urgent prayer for such men and women; paid and unpaid, in secular employment, as mothers and carers at the school gate, as workers in the service industries, as employees of local churches, all labouring for the Lord in whatever situation of life God has placed them.

We need to ask, then, just how deep is our own commitment to personal prayer? Do we really understand the times? We are not simply talking about five minutes squeezed in at the end of a busy day. Instead, a sustained, daily discipline of prayer is what is needed. One friend of mine recently put it like this, 'Christian prayer is not conducted from the comfortable armchair of the contemplative. Christian prayer is done from the edge of a hard seat, straining forward to the promises of God.' Jesus did not consider himself able to engage in God's work meaningfully and to train up labourers if he did not pray. We may feel that we are busy, but Jesus was far busier than any of us could imagine. He was surrounded for most of his ministry by literally thousands of people, all of whom wanted his attention, moment by moment through the day. Even so, he managed to prioritise, because he had a clear-headed conviction about the times in which we live. If Jesus needed to set a premium on time given up to pray, then certainly we need to do the same.

As I prepared this study I had in mind the prayer diary for one area of the ministry at our church. It is designed for the work amongst City workers, so we call it 'The Prayer Broker'. One day is given over to praying for one of the largest insurance houses in the world. There is a small group of 5 to 10 men and women there who are praying earnestly for the Lord to send out labourers into the harvest field of their offices. The next day we shall be praying for a medium-sized investment house, where a little group have been praying earnestly for the Lord to advance the work of thrusting labourers into the harvest. The day after, the London Bridge Network will be the focus of our prayers, a forum where city workers are seeking to develop a new workplace ministry just south of the river Thames.

As I was thinking about our prayer life, my mind turned to the urgency, commitment and concentration with which our national sportsmen approach their task. As I write, England is currently engaged in a fierce battle with South Africa on the cricket field. As one watches the players in their preparation and performance, there is an element of fervent intensity about all their actions. We could say that they understand the times! How much more then should those who have a true understanding of the days in which we live be marked out by fervent zeal when it comes to their prayer lives?

Do we understand the times? If we do, then we shall see that it is a day for clear-headed kingdom conviction, and for gut-wrenching compassion. The mark of our level of understanding will lie in our personal and corporate commitment to prayer, as we ask the Lord to thrust out labourers into his harvest.

Suggested Questions for group or personal study

1. Spend five minutes doing a personal, and honest, analysis of how much time you spend in personal prayer each day. Describe to yourself the nature of the intensity of the experience.

2. What evidence can you observe of a breakdown in our national life? How do you feel about it?

3. Verse 35 provides a summary of one theme from chapters 8 and 9. What does it remind us of concerning Jesus' identity? How have each of the incidents in chapter 8 and 9 made the same point?

4. Verse 36 also provides a summary of one theme from chapters 8 and 9. What have we seen in these chapters that has provoked the compassion of Jesus?

5. Look up Numbers 27 verses 16-17; 1 Kings 22 verse 17; Psalm 23 verse 1; and Ezekiel 34 verses 16 and 23-24. How do these passages help us understand Matthew 9 verse 36 better?

6. How does the True Shepherd of God's sheep respond to his people as he sees them living out their lives in a fallen world? Consider your responses to question 2 (above). In what way does Jesus' response challenge our response to people in our fallen society? If we truly understand the times, how ought we to respond?

7. Read verse 37 carefully. What does this verse tell us should be the response of someone who feels godly compassion for the lost?

8. Look back at your answer to question 1 (above). What does this tell you about how well you understand the times?

9. What *precisely* does Jesus tell us to pray for in verses 37-38? What is assumed, what is needed?

10. What practical steps do you need to take concerning this week's diary if you are going to obey Jesus?

Preacher's Note 1

Some people suggest that Matthew 9 verse 35 is an 'inclusio' with Matthew 4 verse 23-25. This suggestion results in a preaching unit running from chapter 4 verse 23 to chapter 9 verse 35. I am not convinced that there is sufficient additional evidence to re-structure the early part of the gospel around these two sections. It is equally likely that Matthew is using these two passages as a simple summary of Jesus' Kingly ministry, first to announce his Kingdom, secondly to proclaim his Arrival. It may also be the case that Matthew repeats the language of chapter 4 verse 23 in order to indicate a similar shift from narrative to discourse and so to set the pattern for the rest of the gospel. John does a similar thing in chapter 4 of his gospel in order to alert his readers to the significance of the signs in the structure of the gospel (see *Read Mark Learn, notes on John* published by Christian Focus).

FIVE

Understanding the Terms of the Kingdom

Matthew 10:1-33

[1]And he called to him his twelve disciples and gave them authority over unclean spirits, to cast them out, and to heal every disease and every affliction. [2]The names of the twelve apostles are these: first, Simon, who is called Peter, and Andrew his brother; James the son of Zebedee, and John his brother; [3]Philip and Bartholomew; Thomas and Matthew the tax collector; James the son of Alphaeus, and Thaddaeus; [4]Simon the Cananaean, and Judas Iscariot, who betrayed him. [5]These twelve Jesus sent out, instructing them, "Go nowhere among the Gentiles and enter no town of the Samaritans, [6]but go rather to the lost sheep of the house of Israel. [7]And proclaim as you go, saying, 'The kingdom of heaven is at hand.' [8]Heal the sick, raise the dead, cleanse lepers, cast out demons. You received without paying; give without pay. [9]Acquire no gold nor silver nor copper for your belts, [10]no bag for your journey, nor two tunics nor sandals nor a staff, for the labourer deserves his food. [11]And whatever town or village you enter, find out who is worthy

in it and stay there until you depart. [12]As you enter the house, greet it. [13]And if the house is worthy, let your peace come upon it, but if it is not worthy, let your peace return to you. [14]And if anyone will not receive you or listen to your words, shake off the dust from your feet when you leave that house or town. [15]Truly, I say to you, it will be more bearable on the day of judgment for the land of Sodom and Gomorrah than for that town. [16]Behold, I am sending you out as sheep in the midst of wolves, so be wise as serpents and innocent as doves. [17]Beware of men, for they will deliver you over to courts and flog you in their synagogues, [18]and you will be dragged before governors and kings for my sake, to bear witness before them and the Gentiles. [19]When they deliver you over, do not be anxious how you are to speak or what you are to say, for what you are to say will be given to you in that hour. [20]For it is not you who speak, but the Spirit of your Father speaking through you. [21]Brother will deliver brother over to death, and the father his child, and children will rise against parents and have them put to death, [22]and you will be hated by all for my name's sake. But the one who endures to the end will be saved. [23]When they persecute you in one town, flee to the next, for truly, I say to you, you will not have gone through all the towns of Israel before the Son of Man comes. [24]A disciple is not above his teacher, nor a servant above his master. [25]It is enough for the disciple to be like his teacher, and the servant like his master. If they have called the master of the house Beelzebul, how much more will they malign those of his household. [26]So have no fear of them, for nothing is covered that will not be revealed, or hidden that will not be known. [27]What I tell you in the dark, say in the light, and what you hear whispered, proclaim on the housetops. [28]And do not fear those who kill the body but cannot kill the soul. Rather fear him who can destroy both soul and body in hell. [29]Are not two sparrows sold for a penny? And not one of them will fall to the ground apart from your Father. [30]But even the hairs of your head are all numbered. [31]Fear not, therefore; you are of more value than many sparrows. [32]So everyone who acknowledges me before men, I also will acknowledge before my Father who is in heaven, [33]but whoever denies me before men, I also will deny before my Father who is in heaven."

In the last chapter, we saw that the times in which we live require clear-headed conviction, for Jesus the Good Shepherd has arrived, the Christ has come. Furthermore, we saw that the times in which we live demand gut-wrenching kingdom compassion, for we live in a world that is under God's judgment. As we see the effects of God's judgment in a fallen world, the genuinely godly response is one of gut-wrenching compassion rather than finger-wagging moral high-horsemanship. We also saw that true Christ-like compassion will be evidenced by serious and sustained prayer for the Lord to send out labourers into his harvest field.

Having commanded his disciples to pray, Jesus immediately set about commissioning and sending his twelve apostles. He had just made it clear that he had come to earth as God's promised king, so it was only logical for Jesus to send out his disciples to proclaim this message in response to their own prayers. When we pray in obedience to Jesus' command, we need to be aware that we too may sometimes be thrust out to answer those prayers! However, as we turn to Matthew 10 verses 1-15, we need to recognise that care is required as we consider their implications for mission.

There is much about Jesus' commissioning of the twelve that was unique to them. It was clearly a specific time, as Jesus, God's King, came to Israel at a specific point in history and declared to his chosen people, the Jews, that he had arrived. That much is immediately apparent from verses 5, 9 and 14. The twelve were being sent only to Israel ('Go nowhere among the Gentiles and enter no town of the Samaritans.'), but by the end of the gospel, Jesus was telling his disciples to go to all nations (Matthew 28 verses 18-20). This must therefore have been a unique time. Furthermore, we read in verse 9 that Jesus instructed the apostles not to take luggage or supplies with them, because their fellow Jews should meet their needs, welcoming them as God's messengers. Yet towards the end of Luke's gospel, Jesus told them that they ought to take these things (Luke 22 verses 35-38). Once again this suggests that the command here in verse 9 was limited to these twelve apostles. Finally, we read in verse 14 that they were to shake the dust off their feet from any town that didn't accept them and move on quickly to another town, yet in Acts the disciples deliberately set up churches in towns and villages, even in places where the apostle Paul was rejected (see Acts 13 and 14). For instance, Paul was driven out of Pisidian Antioch, Iconium and Lystra, yet other disciples remained in these places establishing churches (Acts 16 verses 2-3). So we need to acknowledge that there is much about this passage that is unique to the apostles.

The signs and wonders that Jesus gave his apostles authority to perform are a case in point. They deliberately paralleled the healing of *every* disease and *every* sickness in chapter 9 verse 35, where the healing ministry of Jesus indicated that God's King had arrived:

> Jesus went throughout all the cities and villages, teaching in their synagogues and proclaiming the gospel of the kingdom and healing every disease and every affliction.

As Jesus called his apostles to him in chapter 10 verse 1, he gave them similar authority over unclean spirits, to cast them out, and to heal *every* disease and *every* affliction. There is a deliberate parallel here to show that this was a specific time and that these apostles were being given a specific commission to announce that God's long-awaited King had arrived to save God's chosen people. So then, these signs and wonders are of a totally different order to the spiritual gifts that are described in the Corinthian church (see 1 Corinthians 12–14). We need to be clear that there is much that is specific, and that we should not expect to replicate what occurs in the ministry of these twelve foundational figures, because they were sent to Israel with a particular task at a particular point in history. (Preacher's Note 1)

However, at another level, there must be some things about the ministry of the twelve that every believer is meant to copy, for at the end of the gospel (chapter 28 verses 18-20) Jesus told his apostles to teach new believers:

> "to observe *all* that I have commanded you."

This helps to explain why, as chapter 10 develops, we see that Jesus has broadened and expanded the horizon to include all disciples everywhere. By verse 24 he is speaking about discipleship generally and not just about the ministry of the twelve:

> "a disciple is not above his teacher, nor a servant above his master."

The same is true in verse 32 ('everyone *who acknowledges...*') and in verses 37-39 Jesus uses the all-encompassing 'whoever' no fewer than five times in the three verses, thus showing that he has every believer in mind. Perhaps the best way to summarise the distinction between what is specific to the apostles and what is not, is to say that the *role* of apostle is unique, but that the apostolic *ministry* of proclaiming the arrival of the kingdom is for everyone.

Widespread proclamation with mixed reception

This apostolic ministry of widespread proclamation is spelled out in verse 7:

> "Proclaim as you go, saying, 'The kingdom of heaven is at hand.'"

Once again this tells us about the times in which we live. The time in which we live is a time for proclamation when, in the language of verse 27, God's people should be shouting from the rooftops what they have heard in secret. As we see from the anticipated reactions described in verses 14 and 15, however, this ministry is not only one of public proclamation, it is also potentially divisive:

> "If anyone will not receive you or listen to your words, shake off the dust from your feet ... it will be more bearable on the day of judgment for the land of Sodom and Gomorrah than for that town."

As the gospel is proclaimed, so it is announced that Jesus Christ, God's King, has arrived. The proclamation of the gospel insists that the time has come to repent, to turn around and to submit to the rule of Jesus. As a person obeys the command to turn to Christ, he or she finds that Jesus offers forgiveness, because *'the Son of Man has authority on earth to forgive sins'* (Matthew 9:6). However, as another person rejects and disobeys the command of Jesus to *'follow me'*, so a division occurs, and that person takes one more step towards ultimate condemnation by Jesus on the day when he returns to destroy all evil. This means that the time has come for widespread, divisive proclamation.

This aspect of apostolic ministry needs to be restated in every generation. There are some today who would hold that the task of outreach is done without the proclamation of the word. They suggest that provided we show by our actions that Jesus loves people, then the work of the gospel is being done. Recently a campaign was run in London that was designed to show the love of Jesus to the people of our city. The vast majority of things that happened in 'Love London' had little to do with public, verbal proclamation. People had their cars washed, their streets swept and their neighbourhoods lovingly cleaned, but in many cases they did not hear the truth proclaimed that *'the kingdom of heaven is at hand'*, nor did they hear the command to repent and turn to follow the King. The campaign was undeniably well intentioned and immensely worthy. However, when Jesus commands us, "proclaim *as you go, saying, 'The kingdom of heaven is at hand'"*(verse 7) and "*what you I tell you in the dark, say in the light, and what you hear whispered,* proclaim *on the housetops"* (verse 27), his assumption is that people will hear a *verbal* message. This is confirmed in verse 14 when he says, *"if anyone will not receive you or* listen *to your words ..."* .

There was recently a university Christian Union in England that held a mission for their campus at which there were no talks explaining the gospel – we need to be clear that this is not apostolic ministry. The vast majority of the Christian Unions in England are doing a fantastic job in proclaiming from the housetops that God's King has arrived, but unless we keep reminding one another that today is a time of urgent and earnest prayer *and* urgent proclamation, we can rapidly fall into sub-apostolic patterns. There are even some in England now who would hold that it is not the duty of every disciple to be involved in the work of speaking the gospel from the rooftops. However, as we have already noted, Jesus' broadening frame of reference in chapter 10, which eventually includes all disciples, makes it plain that everybody is expected to be involved in this project.

This is confirmed as we look at Matthew's gospel as a whole. Some of Jesus' first words are, *"Follow me, and I will make you fishers of men"* (chapter 4 verse 19). His last words are:

> "Go therefore and make disciples of all nations, baptising them in the name of the Father and of the Son and of the Holy Spirit, teaching them to observe all that I have commanded you."

It is the expectation of Matthew's gospel that all believers should be engaged in the glorious project of widespread proclamation in whatever way is appropriate to each individual's gifts and personality. Certainly that's the way the early church understood it. For instance, we read in Acts 8 verses 1-4:

> And there arose on that day a great persecution against the church in Jerusalem, and they were all scattered throughout

the regions of Judea and Samaria, except the apostles ....
Now those who were scattered went about preaching the
word.

Sociologist Rodney Stark has written a book about the growth of
Christianity, in which he charts the extraordinary advance of the
gospel in the first four centuries of the church's existence. He is
an American academic and I am told that he does not profess to be
a Christian. In his book, *The Rise of Early Christianity,* he has shown
that by 350 AD over 55% of the Roman Empire was made up of
professing Christians. Indeed, Stark insists that despite what many
scholars would have us believe, Emperor Constantine became a
Christian out of political expediency. Once he realised that 55%
of the population were already Christian, he then thought it was
rather a good idea to become a Christian himself. If this is true, it
means that it wasn't Constantine who forced Christianity on the
Roman Empire, but quite the reverse. How did this extraordinary
growth in Christianity happen? Stark cites the loving care and
gospel lifestyle of the early Christian communities. However,
another famous church historian, Adolf Harnack, writing of the
same period, notes the vital ingredient of public proclamation:

> The most numerous and successful missionaries of the
> Christian religion were not the regular teachers, but the
> Christians themselves .... We cannot hesitate to believe
> that the great mission of Christianity was in reality
> accomplished by means of informal missionaries.[1]

In other words, every member and every disciple saw him or
herself as engaged personally in the task of widespread, public
proclamation. Indeed, another church historian, Edward Gibbon,
puts it like this:

---

[1] Adolf Harnack, *The Mission and Expansion of Christianity in the
First Three Centuries* pp. 366-368, published by Harper, 1961

It became the most sacred duty of a new convert to diffuse among his friends and relations the inestimable blessing which he had received.[2]

The early disciples, with their clear-headed conviction and Christ-like compassion, realised that the time had come both for urgent prayer and for widespread, but divisive, public proclamation. They understood the times!

All of this is really the elementary 'ABC' of Christian discipleship. It is the sort of thing that every baby Christian is taught in Christian Basics class. However, it needs to be re-stated in every generation, for if a third or fourth generation of Christians reaches a point where they feel that they have outgrown a discipleship that involves sustained prayer and continued proclamation, then they will find that they have drifted away from Jesus and from authentic apostolic ministry.

Unprovoked persecution with heavenly provision

Having spelled out for us the times, Jesus goes on to lay out the terms and conditions of discipleship in his kingdom. Once again the logic of Matthew's gospel is deeply compelling. As Jesus moves on from teaching about the nature of the times in which the disciples were living to explaining the terms and conditions of discipleship, there is no hidden small print! If the time has come for widespread and divisive proclamation, then his followers need to know that their discipleship will inevitably involve persecution.

Verse 16 uses an extraordinary image:

"Behold, I am sending you out as sheep in the midst of wolves, so be wise as serpents and innocent as doves."

I have only once seen a flock of sheep subjected to the teeth of ravenous wolves. Actually, it was a Great Dane and a St Bernard

---

[2] Edward Gibbon, *The Decline and Fall of the Roman Empire*, volume 1, p. 388, published by Random House

that did the damage, but before the farmer had time to reach for his shotgun and deal with the dogs, they had caused irreparable harm. Three sheep had to be shot on the spot, numerous lambs were dead, and the rest of the day was spent with needle and thread trying to sew up the torn skins of the survivors. Now, says Jesus, I am sending you out as sheep in the midst of wolves. In other words Jesus, the Good Shepherd, is deliberately, intentionally and knowingly sending his disciples out on the understanding that the place to which they are going is a place of ravenous wolves. Of course, they are not to be stupid. They are to be *'wise as serpents and innocent as doves';* so they are to be gentle and there is to be no Christian masochism. We are not to stick out our chins, as it were, as Christians, and invite a ravenous wolf to take a bite – any persecution we suffer should be unprovoked. However there will be opposition for those who engage in and line up with genuine Christian ministry, says Jesus, and he is sending his disciples into the teeth of it. The terms and conditions are those of persecution.

Persecution by the state has been a fact of life for the church in many places since its inception. A few years ago I began the year by reading a few pages of *Foxe's Book of Martyrs* to my wife Janet each evening. I'm afraid we didn't get very far, because the staff team at St Helen's suggested that reading a chapter of *Foxe's Book of Martyrs* to her on the evening of our wedding anniversary wasn't altogether the best way to build our marriage! However the *Book of Martyrs* does make salutary reading. The earliest disciples were boiled in oil, tied by their limbs to animals and dragged apart, or (as happened in Nero's day) soaked in wax, tied to posts, and set alight as lamps for his garden. Some had their property removed; many were imprisoned and lost their jobs.

I suspect that many of us (and I speak for myself) secretly harbour in our hearts a longing for a day in this age when the world speaks well of us and in which we will be able to influence the government, the media, the human resources department, the staff room or the university student union in such a way that everybody will rather look forward to our coming to proclaim the message of Jesus. I think some of us (and again I speak for myself) secretly harbour in our hearts a longing for a day when our political manoeuvring amongst the establishment of our nation will be so sophisticated that the movers and shakers of society will skip with delight when they hear that a devoted follower of Jesus, who takes the bible seriously, is coming their way. If we harbour such hopes, then we need to read verse 16 again, carefully: *'Behold, I am sending you out as sheep in the midst of wolves, so be wise as serpents and innocent as doves.'* According to Jesus, no such day exists!

Over the last 150 years, in much of the Western world, we have been wonderfully free from public persecution. To that extent, the times we've been living in have been abnormal for Christian discipleship. Those with any experience of living for Christ in a different culture will be much more realistic and have a far better understanding of the times. We are not being sensationalist when we suggest that the times do appear to be changing back to a more normal state of affairs in our Western culture. Peter Berger has noted that the widespread assumption amongst secularists that 'religion' would die out as modernism advanced, has proved to be misplaced. He writes:

> the world today, with some exceptions … is as furiously religious as it ever was, and in some cases more so. This means that a whole body of literature by historians and social scientists loosely labelled 'secularisation theory' is essentially mistaken … the religious impulse, the quest for meaning that transcends the restricted space of empirical existence in this world has been a perennial feature of humanity … it would require something close to a mutation of the species to extinguish this impulse for good.[3]

---

[3] Peter Berger, *The Desecularisation of the World* pp. 2 and 13, published by Eerdmans 1999

Facing the failure of the liberal-humanist project, secularists have recently become noticeably more aggressive and less 'liberal'. The shrill rantings of Richard Dawkins, Philip Pullman and Christopher Hitchens, for example, are well known. This attitude now spills over into the sphere of our public life more frequently. Melanie Phillips, a columnist in one of Britain's tabloid newspapers, recently published an article entitled: *How Britain is turning Christianity into a crime*. Another tabloid recently published an image of the baby Jesus in a manger with the front page headlines: 'is this the most hated man in Britain?' As Jesus spelled out the terms and conditions of the kingdom, his first headline point was that there would be unprovoked persecution.

Since it is a time for sustained, serious prayer and urgent, widespread proclamation, the terms of the kingdom inevitably involve conditions of unprovoked persecution. However, as Matthew continues with his usual detailed precision, he gives us two parallel subsections (verses 17-20 and 21-23) which unpack and explain the nature of this unprovoked persecution. Each of these subsections has within it both a description of the persecution – first from synagogue and state (verses 17-18), then from friends and family (verses 21-22) – and a promise of God's provision for those who are being persecuted (verses 19-20 and verse 23).

In verses 17-18 we learn that Jesus told his disciples that unprovoked persecution would come not only from the state, but more surprisingly, from the synagogue:

> Beware of men, for they will deliver you over to courts and flog you in their synagogues, and you will be dragged before governors and kings for my sake, to bear witness before them and the Gentiles.

The extraordinary thing here is that the very people whom we might have expected to defend Jesus' disciples, as they proclaimed the truth of the arrival of his kingdom, were precisely the people who persecuted them. Their persecutors were men of the synagogue, who would even go so far as to flog the disciples before dragging them before the Roman governors and kings. So Jesus tells us that it will often be the religious authorities, jealous or fearful of losing their position of acceptance with the secular powers, who initiate persecution of his followers (see John 11 verse 48 and Acts 13 verse 45ff).

Failure to understand this pattern of persecution will result in a sense of confusion for believers when they find religious people persecuting them. Jesus tells us that we are to expect hostility from jealous religious authorities as well as from the state. It is right to say that we have been living in most unusual times in the West during the last few hundred years. Our brothers and sisters in Eastern Europe and communist China have experienced much more 'normal' discipleship than we have.

Once a year I have the privilege of travelling to Riga in Latvia, where our church is in partnership with a number of churches from the Baltic States. On one of my first trips to Riga I was taken to the Museum of Occupation. This museum has preserved a record of the fifty years of occupation of Latvia, first by the Soviets, then by the Nazis, and once again (after the second World War) by the Soviets. Both of these atheistic regimes sought to stamp out genuine Christianity. Sadly, in both instances, it was the case that the national church complied with the state and failed to protect genuine Christians in order to preserve its position. The same, well-documented pattern has been observed in communist China, where biblically faithful disciples are mostly to be found in the 'underground' house churches because of the perceived interference of the state in officially registered churches. Jesus tells us to expect persecution from the religious leaders and suggests that times will come when the religious authorities will hand over true disciples to the state for punishment. It is therefore unlikely that the currently benign environment that exists in the West today will continue forever.

Recently I came across Samuel Huntingdon's book, *The Clash of Civilizations and the Remaking of the World Order*. In it, Huntington notes the pitifully low birth-rates of Western secularist states, which mean that they are forced to encourage and rely on immigration to survive. Personally, I enjoy the rich and diverse cultural melting pot in our urban centres, and I am glad of the opportunities for Christian ministry as the nations are brought to our doorstep here in London. However, as this influx takes place, the incomers are in general not only substantially more religious than the western secularists, they also have far higher birth-rates, and will therefore increase in influence in our societies.

In this new context, true Christians will want to take advantage of the opportunity to proclaim the gospel and declare boldly that Jesus Christ is God's true King and that he alone is King over God's kingdom. In all probability the state will be deeply opposed to such activity, and established religious leaders, if they are not Christian, will seek to create a religion that fits with what the state wants in order not to rock the boat.

You may feel this scenario is unnecessarily alarmist, but in the United Kingdom there have recently been a number of instances where secular-minded university Student Unions have sought to ban the Christian groups on their campus from proclaiming the gospel, on the grounds that it would be contrary to the spirit of diversity and tolerance espoused by the university. In the General Synod of the Church of England there has been considerable controversy recently over a private member's motion seeking to affirm the uniqueness of Jesus Christ as the only way to salvation. In the City of London, amongst the financial institutions, Christians are finding it increasingly difficult to publicise their activities under the new restrictions of 'diversity' legislation.

We can be sure that as we stand firm, and as we continue to proclaim Jesus Christ as the only Lord and Saviour of mankind, then the rest of the 'global village' will hate us. The hottest hostility will come from the religious.

A ruined reputation with heavenly recognition

The next section of chapter 10 is introduced in verses 24 and 25 by the second, but not yet the most shocking, of the three big statements that Jesus uses to introduce the three major sections of this chapter. Before we study the verses closely, it is worth considering the question: what adjectives would you expect to be used to describe a person who is genuinely like Jesus? No doubt the list would include such words as loving, joyful, peaceable and patient. I suspect that very few would answer the question using the categories of verses 24 to 25:

> "A disciple is not above his teacher, nor a servant above his master. It is enough for the disciple to be like his teacher, and the servant like his master. If they have called the master of the house Beelzebul, how much more will they malign those of his household."

If to be like Jesus is to be accused of being of the devil, then to be godly is to have a ruined reputation. In other words, just as the terms of belonging to the kingdom involve unprovoked persecution, so they also involve having a ruined reputation. Jesus is not suggesting that we should be so provocative and so deliberately obtuse and obnoxious that everybody hates us. Nor would he commend a ruined reputation gained as a result of ungodly behaviour or incompetent professional performance. Nonetheless, as we engage in urgent prayer and divisive proclamation, which are the activities of true compassion, then people are going to accuse us of being of the devil himself.

I fear this comes as something of a surprise to us, because we secretly hope that there will be a day when everybody will speak well of Christians or when the proclamation of the gospel in our locality will be universally welcomed. We need to realise that no such time exists. When I first prepared to preach on this passage, I decided to make a list of some of the things that bible-believing, bible-teaching men and women have been called in the Press in recent times. Here is the list: 'The Al-Qaeda of the Church of England'; 'the mullahs of the Christian faith'; 'bigots, hypocrites, totally un-Christian'; 'smugly pious'; 'institutionally homophobic'; 'sexist, racist, and rich'.

Sometimes I suspect that we are in danger of falling into the trap of thinking that we Christians would be more universally popular if only our church leaders employed full time media consultants or, perhaps, if our leaders were not quite so blunt, or if those who spoke about Jesus publicly were a touch more sophisticated. These verses suggest that if we really do think that there will be a day when we will wake up to hear the current affairs team of our national radio station speaking well of our Christian leaders, then we may well find that our Christian leaders have so changed the message of Jesus that they are no longer following the true Jesus of the bible. The terms and conditions of the kingdom include a ruined reputation.

Here is a small personal test of godliness for us: the next time we find ourselves reading an article in a newspaper in which a public Christian leader is facing abuse on the grounds of proclaiming the truth of Jesus' kingdom, let's pause and listen to our own thoughts. If we find ourselves saying, 'I really appreciate X, but I wish …,' we need to ask ourselves whether we are really saying, 'I wish he wasn't so like Jesus'.

Matthew moves on in verses 26 to 33 to record a number of reasons why disciples should continue to engage in divisive proclamation of the gospel in spite of the hostility they face. There are three great incentives, and each of them is future-focused. Once again, this presents a challenge to anyone who believes that the benefits of belonging to Jesus come to us primarily in the here and now. These verses suggest to us that the vast majority of the benefits of following Jesus will be realised in the future. Those who expound a so-called 'gospel' of 'health and prosperity now' certainly do not dwell on Jesus' insistence that unprovoked persecution and ruined reputation will characterise his followers. Their incentives for discipleship are largely wrapped up in this world. Jesus' are not.

The three 'have no fear' statements in verses 26, 28 and 31 speak of heavenly recognition for Jesus' followers. They are brought together and summed up in verses 32 and 33. The first incentive speaks of **heavenly vindication** (verses 26-27):

> "So have no fear of them, for nothing is covered that will not be revealed, or hidden that will not be known. What I tell you in the dark, say in the light, and what you hear whispered, proclaim on the housetops."

On the final day, when Jesus returns, everything will be made clear. There is nothing new here that we have not already covered in the first four chapters of this book, for if we have a clear-headed understanding of the times in which we live, we will know that Jesus has come as King, that he has died for sin, is enthroned in heaven as the Son of Man, and will return in glory to destroy all evil and to bring his new heaven and new earth. Therefore, since 'nothing is covered that will not be revealed, or hidden that will not be known' we need have no fear now as we proclaim Jesus Christ as Lord, for on the last day when everything will be laid bare and brought into the open, all Jesus' disciples will be seen to have been on the winning side. This is the language of **heavenly vindication.**

Those who are familiar with the English soccer scene will know that there is a team in England called Manchester United. One of their supporters' anthems is: 'Glory, glory, Man United!' Wherever you find the team playing, there you will hear this accompaniment! I sometimes ask myself, why is it that their fans are prepared to go on chanting this mantra wherever we find them? The answer is that they genuinely believe they will be vindicated at the end of the season. Infuriatingly, more often than not they are! So they go on with their public proclamation, singing from the rooftops in spite of hostile opposition.

How much more, when the stakes are so much higher and the confidence so much greater, should we continue with the proclamation of the glorious truth of the gospel. On the final day, everything will be laid bare and heavenly vindication will be ours. People may laugh at us in the office, they may mock us in our family, they may even threaten us and our parents may begin to hate us; we may have our reputation ruined, and we may be unjustly accused of any number of things. However, if we understand the times in which we live, we will realise that Jesus is God's King and that nothing is covered that will not be revealed.

The second '*fear not*' comes in verse 28 and speaks of **hellish damnation:**

> "Do not fear those who kill the body but cannot kill the soul. Rather fear him who can destroy both soul and body in hell."

This will appear to many to be a most unusual incentive, but it will only seem unusual to those who have failed to meditate sufficiently on the realities of the times in which we live. If we understand the times, we will know the lessons of chapter 8 and 9. We will realise that when he comes, Jesus will utterly destroy all God's enemies. He has already shown us that he is God's King, and therefore we would be wise to examine the relative power of the two forces that we are likely to fear. If we are more tempted to fear our manager in the office or our colleagues, the peer group in our university campus or staff room, then we need to learn to fear the Lord much, much more. After all, he will utterly destroy all his enemies on the last day. So the incentive here is that of hellish destruction. Fear of hell is a great incentive to us to engage boldly in the proclamation of the gospel. Do not fear men, for they will be utterly destroyed by Jesus if they continue in their foolish opposition to him.

Finally, it's worth going on sharing the good news of Jesus with our friends and colleagues and proclaiming it publicly *'from the rooftops'*, because of the *'fear not'* in verse 29. The two illustrations in these verses speak of **heavenly recognition**:

> "Are not two sparrows sold for a penny? And not one of them will fall to the ground apart from your Father. But even the hairs of your head are all numbered. Fear not, therefore; you are of more value than many sparrows. So everyone who acknowledges me before men, I also will acknowledge before my Father who is in heaven, but whoever denies me before men, I also will deny before my Father who is in heaven."

The point here is that our death will not catch God by surprise. He knows every detail about us, he is watching over us; when we finally do die, it will not be a shock to God. The first illustration is of the sparrow whose market value in our culture, as in first century Israel, is next to nil. Even though the sparrow is of such little value, the Lord in heaven knows the precise moment when each one drops to the ground. The second illustration of hairs falling to the ground is of slightly less consolation to some of us than to others! The point of both illustrations is that no man or woman's death will catch God by surprise. God knows the precise circumstances of each one of his people; he loves each one, he cares for each one, and we matter to him more than a million sparrows or any number of hairs. As verses 32 and 33 point out, those who acknowledge God's beloved Son before men on earth, will be greeted with the unimaginably joyful privilege of being acknowledged by the only one who matters in heaven.

As we close this chapter, it is worth considering the scene at the end of our lives as we return home to be with the Lord of heaven and earth. I occasionally attend receptions in the City of London where executives of big organisations and businesses are present. I have often observed how there is always something of a scrum around the person who is considered to matter most. Everybody wants to shake hands with the most important person in the room, and there is almost always a group of people trying to get near to the man or woman with the greatest influence. When we die, whether suddenly and unexpectedly, or slowly and after long preparation, we shall find ourselves brought before the Lord and Creator of the heavens and earth. At that moment, there will be only one person in the whole universe who matters. The King of kings and Lord of lords has promised that he will greet each one of his people and bring each one face-to-face with their Father in heaven. We shall be *'acknowledged'* – greeted as a long-awaited family member – by the only one who counts. The prospect of the opposite happening is unimaginably wretched.

Suggested Questions for group or personal study

1. When you hear that a friend or colleague has become a Christian, what do you consider will be the result for them in terms of their public image, their family relationships, their career and future prospects? Why do you think Christians in your country, in general, get such a bad press?

2. What indication is there that aspects of Jesus' teaching in chapter 10 verses 1-15 are for the twelve apostles alone?

3. What aspects of chapter 10 verses 1-15 apply to all believers? (you may need to read the first few pages of the study to help you with this question.)

4. What would you say to a person who suggests: 'I don't need to speak to my friends about Jesus, all that matters is the life that I lead'?

5. How does what Jesus says in verses 16-23 match up to your answer from question 1 (above)?

6. What is surprising about the *source* of persecution in verses 17-18 and verses 21-22? What provision is there for those who are hated?

7. How does what Jesus says in verses 24-25 match up to your answer from question 1? What is the logic of verses 24-25?

8. How would you respond to someone who insists that a Christian will find people respect them and speak highly of them because of their Christian witness?

9. How does what Jesus says in verses 26-33 serve to encourage the person whose reputation has been ruined through following Jesus? Why do you think we might find the encouragement of verse 28 so surprising? If we do find it surprising, what does that suggest about us?

10. Where does the focus of the encouragement in verses 26-33 lie? What does this tell us about the nature of Christian discipleship?

Preacher's Note 1

I quote here from an email correspondence with Ben Cooper, who is currently researching a PhD thesis in Matthew's gospel. The discussion that initiated the following comments from him had to do with what is, and what is not, directly applicable to us from Matthew 10 verses 1-15. 'The one-sentence answer is: reading chapter 10 through the 'lens' of the death and resurrection of Jesus shows us what does and what does not apply to us as instruction, and the more we re-read the Gospel, the sharper into focus that will become.

Having said that, even a new reader will see that Matthew is bending over backwards to set at least the initial instruction in chapter 10 as specific to the twelve [apostles] (even to the extent of listing them by name), for a specific purpose (the mission only to Israel) and for a specific time-frame (chapter 10 verse 23).

A reader more familiar with Matthew will also recognise chapter 10 verses 1 and 8 as pre-resurrection proclamation of the Kingdom; that is, pre-resurrection ministry. The healing and exorcism miracles in the synoptics are pictures of resurrection: the nearness of the Kingdom is expressed as people are rescued from the shadow of death (cf chapter 4 verse 16). This is particularly true of 'raising the dead' (chapter 10 verse 8) of course! In this the twelve are simply multiplying what Jesus has been doing. But that ministry is of course overshadowed and supplanted once the disciples have seen the event those miracles pointed to: the risen Lord, given all authority (chapter 28 verse 18). It's after having seen the resurrection that the disciples are called upon to go and make disciples of all nations. In other words, the greater testimony of news of the risen Lord overshadows the lesser testimony of miracles like those in chapter 9 verse 8 and chapter 10 verses 1 and 8.

What's more, as a reader gets even more familiar with Matthew's Gospel, he will begin to recognise the ways in which other parts of chapter 10 apply to his situation. Although there are differences between the mission to Israel and the mission to the nations (brought about by the death and resurrection of Jesus), there are parallels too. Chapter 10 verse 18 seems especially directed to a post-resurrection situation. In other words, as the chapter progresses, Matthew is saying: as Jesus said to the twelve concerning openness, persecution, perseverance etc in their mission, so he says to you in yours. The situations are parallel.'

SIX

Understanding the Ties of the Kingdom

Matthew 10:34-42

³⁴"Do not think that I have come to bring peace to the earth. I have not come to bring peace, but a sword. ³⁵For I have come to set a man against his father, and a daughter against her mother, and a daughter-in-law against her mother-in-law. ³⁶And a person's enemies will be those of his own household. ³⁷Whoever loves father or mother more than me is not worthy of me, and whoever loves son or daughter more than me is not worthy of me. ³⁸And whoever does not take his cross and follow me is not worthy of me. ³⁹Whoever finds his life will lose it, and whoever loses his life for my sake will find it. ⁴⁰Whoever receives you receives me, and whoever receives me receives him who sent me. ⁴¹The one who receives a prophet because he is a prophet will receive a prophet's reward, and the one who receives a righteous person because he is a righteous person will receive a righteous person's reward. ⁴²And whoever gives one of these little ones even a cup of cold water because he is a disciple, truly, I say to you, he will by no means lose his reward."

I have given this chapter the title 'Understanding the Ties of the Kingdom' and we shall be examining the networks and connections of Christian disciples, seeking to answer the questions: 'where should our loyalties lie if we are Christians?' and 'what will being a member of God's kingdom do to our relationships?'

Changed family relationships

First, in verses 34 and 35, we discover that if we understand the times in which we live, then belonging to the kingdom of Jesus will bring a change in family relations. These verses contain the most shocking of all the shocking things that Jesus has to say to us in this chapter:

> "Do not think that I have come to bring peace to the earth. I have not come to bring peace, but a sword. For I have come to set a man against his father, and a daughter against her mother, and a daughter-in-law against her mother-in-law. And a person's enemies will be those of his own household."

A friend of my mother was seeing her daughter-in-law off at Gatwick. It had not been a pleasant visit because they didn't get on well, and as she helped her daughter-in-law onto the bus that was to carry her into the airport, the mother-in-law finally lost it. Standing in the bus, with all the other passengers listening, she said at the top of her voice, 'You are a lazy and selfish slut, you never lift a finger to help anybody, you never think of anybody apart from yourself, you have ruined my son. Go back to America and I hope you never return.'

There are all sorts of reasons why a mother-in-law may not get on well with her daughter-in-law, but Jesus says in verses 34-35 that if we understand the times of the kingdom, and if we understand the terms of the kingdom, many of us may well find that there will be changes in our family ties, and in our networks and connections. At the heart of such changes will be not a daughter-in-law's habits in the home of her mother-in-law, or a son's frustration with his father's stubborn conservatism, or a father's irritation at the behaviour of his son – rather the change in attitude will be due to a son's commitment to Jesus, a mother's proclamation of Jesus or a child's determination to announce the kingdom of Christ from the rooftops and to structure his or her priorities around the fact that Jesus is the King. The coming of Jesus will bring a sword into the heart of families.

Jesus' statement, *'I am sending you out as sheep in the midst of wolves'* (chapter 10 verse 16), was one of the most shocking things he said in his entire public ministry. Telling his disciples that they were likely to be called Beelzebul, or Satan (verses 24-25) was equally disturbing. Most shocking of all, however, was Jesus' suggestion in verses 34-36 that his coming could mean his followers arriving home one day to find enemies amongst their own family. Once again, this is hardly the prosperity gospel of health and wealth that so many teach today. As we work through this study, we shall see just how far those who teach such a message have strayed from the true teaching of the historical Jesus. Indeed, these verses challenge the popular understanding of the person of Jesus Christ so deeply that I have sometimes considered using them for a carol service text! (You will be glad to know that I have not yet had the courage to do so!)

In the Western church, where we have had so little experience of persecution, we tend to find these verses hard to grasp. Those from other cultures have no such problems. I was speaking on this passage on a Sunday morning recently when three Chinese adults were baptised. For them, the prospect of their Christian conversion being discovered by the Communist party filled them with fear. They knew that becoming a true follower of Jesus would radically impact their networks and connections. One recent Sunday in St Helen's we had the joy of baptising both a young man from a strong Jewish background and a girl from a radical feminist background. It was wonderful to see two people from such different faith systems turning to follow Jesus. Both the woman, with her background of secular materialist faith, and the Jew, with his background of religious faith, spoke of the cost of believing in Jesus in terms of family connections. A young Muslim convert I know had to flee his country of birth when he became a Christian, because his brother had issued a death threat against him. As we examine these verses, we realise that those of us in the West who follow Jesus, and yet have been free from radical changes in our networks and connections, have been living in most unusual times.

Changed family values

So why is it that our networks and connections are likely to be changed so substantially as we follow Jesus? The answer lies in the second point that Jesus made, found in verses 37-39, which is that this change in family relations comes as a result of a change in family values. Notice how tightly they are focused on Jesus:

> "Whoever loves father or mother more than me is not worthy of me, and whoever loves son or daughter more than me is not worthy of me. And whoever does not take his cross and follow me is not worthy of me. Whoever finds his life will lose it, and whoever loses his life for my sake will find it."

As we study these verses, I hope you will be persuaded that they explain why the changes described in verses 35 and 36 come about.

When we read the technical commentaries on these verses, almost all of them suggest that Matthew has drawn together a fairly random collection of Jesus' sayings that are roughly on the same theme. The suggestion is even made by some that Matthew had these additional sentences of Jesus in his collection and he put them here because he couldn't think where else to put them! Whenever I hear someone say something like that, it always makes me suspicious. (Preacher's Note 1) After all, we have already noticed just how careful and concise a writer Matthew is. The organisation and logic of his gospel is relentlessly rigorous, so it would be completely out of character for Matthew to put something into his gospel without a very specific reason.

The whole purpose of this second section of Matthew's gospel has been to show us that Jesus, God's King, has arrived. Every title given to him through this section makes the point: he is the Lord who has come in majesty to rule God's new creation; he is the Son of God, God's King, who has come in power to destroy evil; he is the Son of Man, the final judge and ruler of all, who will be given an everlasting dominion, with every tribe and nation worshipping him; he is the Son of David, God's King; he is the Bridegroom who has come to bring in the glorious banquet. Therefore those who understand the times in which we live, realising who Jesus is, will readjust all of their priorities, goals and ambitions around Jesus Christ because they love Jesus with all their heart, all their mind, all their soul and all their strength. This radical re-shaping of their values will inevitably bring a change in their networks and relationships.

Once we grasp this point, the logic of these verses is not hard to follow. I spoke on this idea of a change of values and change of relationships in South Africa shortly after the English cricket team had won a series of cricket matches there, and decided to use the cricketing career of Kevin Pietersen as an illustration. Pietersen was born in South Africa and he used to play for the Dolphins of Natal. So there was a time when he wore the light and dark green of Natal Province and was hitting sixes and centuries for them. I said, 'We're all used to the kind of hostility that is provoked through someone changing their allegiance. Think, for example, of Kevin Pietersen' (who had been the lead run scorer in the series of matches). 'There was a time when he was proud to don the light and dark green of Natal Province, and to hit sixes and centuries for them. Then he saw the light, and within no time, he was standing with the best of them, singing, "God save our gracious Queen" and hitting sixes and centuries for the English.' Within thirty seconds, people in the congregation were actually hissing and booing! The thought of someone so changing their values as to abandon what their culture held dear, and to adopt another nationality, was so deeply offensive that they just couldn't help themselves. How much more so when someone turns back to God! The bible tells us that the unbelieving family of that man and woman hates God, seeks to suppress the knowledge of God, and hides from God (John 7 verse 7; Romans 1 verse 21; John 3 verse 20). It is not surprising, then, that an unbelieving family will find the presence of a godly disciple a constant sore and a regular reminder of their own wilful rebellion against Jesus Christ and their ultimate destiny. A sword will be brought into such a family through the change in family values of the new convert.

Changed family values: A new first love

Jesus unpacks those new values in three different ways, beginning in verse 37 with the new love.

> "Whoever loves father or mother more than me is not worthy of me, and whoever loves son or daughter more than me is not worthy of me."

As we examine this statement, it is clear that the doctrine of the cross lies behind it. Having seen the love of Jesus, the Christian man or woman who has been brought into Jesus' family cannot but respond by loving Jesus Christ as his or her first love above all else. We saw in chapters 8 and 9 that Jesus is not only the King of kings, but also the suffering servant who has come with all of God's authority to die on the cross, to forgive sins and to summon sinners (8 verse 17; 9 verses 6 and 9). As Christian disciples meditate on the cross of Christ, they will find that they cannot but love Jesus above all other things.

Consider Matthew for a moment. As Matthew stood at the foot of the cross watching Jesus die in his place, he must have remembered that he was once a sinner, living his life with no reference to God at all, deserving nothing less than God's condemnation. He had been spiritually dead, powerless, blind and deaf to God's voice. He had followed the prince of this world and had set his course on a path that was diametrically opposed to God. As he gazed at Jesus hanging on the cross, he saw the Lord of lords and King of kings, whose hands had 'flung stars into space'[1]. Now those same hands were nailed to the tree for his sake. The one who was 'rich beyond all splendour'[2] had, for Matthew's sake, become poorer than the poorest beggar. He existed before all things – 'without him was not any thing made that was made' (John chapter 1 verse 3); he was 'the image of the invisible God, the firstborn of all creation' (Colossians 1 verse 15), the exact representation of God's being (Hebrews 1:3). Yet out of his love for sinners like Matthew, the Son of Man had come with all of God's authority on earth, to be nailed to a cross, to carry God's judgment and wrath at the sin of the whole world. Matthew's sentiments must at least have echoed the words of Isaac Watts' great hymn: 'love so amazing, so divine demands my soul, my life, my all.'[3] In other words, such amazing love should evoke a devotion which, when a choice has to be made, will take precedence over family ties. For whoever loves family relatives above the God who made us and died on a cross for us, has failed to grasp who Jesus is and what Jesus has done. The times in which we live demand a new first love.

Notice, the point here is *not* that Christians will cease to love their father or mother, their son or daughter. There is to be no change to the fifth commandment. So we ought not to pick up the telephone after

---

[1] *From heaven he came* by Graham Kendrick
[2] *Thou who wast rich* by Frank Houghton
[3] *When I survey the wondrous cross*

reading this chapter and ring up our parents in order to announce that we no longer love them! The point is that we should obey the first and greatest commandment: to love the Lord our God with all our heart, mind, soul and strength. To obey this commandment is to make Jesus our primary focus. As we do so, the other commandments will fall into place, and we will find that we are a better father, mother, son or daughter than we ever knew we could be.

However, in a godless, secular culture, as a child who loves Jesus first starts to put the priority of gospel proclamation on his or her agenda, the idea that children could love their Creator more than their parents will often bring real conflict within a godless family. When the parents of one young man I know began to see the implications of his new discipleship, they sat him down and lectured him on all that they had done for him through his life, and then finished their lecture with the words: 'we did not spend all of that for you to do this.' Another young man was disinherited by his father when he turned to Christ. In many cases the change in family relations will be nothing like so dramatic; nonetheless, we should not be surprised to find our relationships with our siblings, parents and even our children impacted as we begin to grow in our love for Jesus. Indeed, it is not just parents who react against children as they turn to follow Jesus. Children can also respond negatively to their parents' desire to put Jesus first. It is not hard to see how a child who has grown up in a Christian home might start to begrudge his godly parents' lifestyle should that child disown the Lord Jesus on reaching adulthood.

The first cause of a change in family relations will be a change in family values that comes from a new first love.

Changed family values: A new first loyalty

Secondly, there will be a change in family values because of a new first loyalty. This point is made by Jesus in verse 38 by using the graphic picture of the cross:

"And whoever does not take his cross and follow me is not worthy of me."

The cross was an object of torture and death, so to say that we must take up our cross is the equivalent today of saying that we must take up our electric chair, or our hangman's noose, or our lethal injection. We need to be clear that Jesus is not suggesting that we should strap a bag of plastic explosives to our body and head off on a suicide mission. Any religion or religious leader who encourages that sort of thing is expounding a satanic doctrine. Jesus is really saying that his disciples are to put self to death as they put into practice in their daily lives what they say they believe with their lips. Living for self is the thing that Jesus hates, because it is at the heart of all sin, and the reason why Jesus had to go to the cross. He died to put an end to me living for me in God's world.

Many of us who have lived through the late twentieth century will have stood in the shower at some point of our lives singing at the top of our voice, 'I did it my way'. The music to Frank Sinatra's song is brilliant and it is not surprising that it has been such a hit. However, whilst the music is great, the lyrics that so captivated the post-1960's generation are as deeply offensive to God in their sentiment as they are expressive of a generation's rejection of God. 'Me doing it my way' is just what the serpent suggested so seductively to Eve in the garden. It is what provokes the just judgment and wrath of God, and it is what took Jesus to his death on my behalf. For the man or woman who has turned to follow Jesus, 'me doing it my way' is now a thing of the past; it has to be killed off even as it was nailed to the cross with Jesus when he went to his death in my place.

This language of putting to death is very graphic. Friends came to us for lunch recently on Christmas Eve. I have to say that at first my children appeared somewhat doubtful about them coming. Their reluctance evaporated as soon as the man, who was from New Zealand, started to talk about his childhood. His opening conversational gambit with the boys ran like this: 'As a child, I used to hunt pigs.' I wish you could have seen two pairs of eyes light up! 'What with?' one boy asked, 'a rifle?' 'No' came the response, 'a knife.' 'What kind of pigs?' 'Wild ones.' 'How big?' 'The biggest was about 700 pounds.' Apparently, he and his friends used to lie on low branches of the trees and jump down on the back of a wild pig and plunge a knife into it. There are now two small boys living in south London who carry in their heads a somewhat tarnished image of all men from New Zealand!

Christians are to carry the image of the cross not just in their heads, but in their whole being. It is an image that speaks of putting a brutal end to me living for me.

Once again, it's not hard to see how a person might be hated for living in such a way, even in their own family. One of the marks of the secularist agenda of the last fifty years has been a revolution that puts 'me' and my freedom to make choices at the heart of the culture's decision-making process – choices that suit me and bring pleasure to me and my family. As we listen to the secularists, we hear them speak in terms of *my* career, *my* possessions, *my* time, *my* ambition, *my* pleasure, *my* portfolio, *my* superannuation fund, *my* freedom, *my* rights, *my* retirement, *my* holidays. Our culture has enshrined living for *me* as one of its key commandments. 'I'll Do It My Way' follows hot on the heels of, 'You shall love *yourself* with all your heart, mind, soul, and strength.' It is not hard to see how disciples of Jesus will prove challenging and uncomfortable to live with as they seek to put to death 'me living for me', and seek instead to live for the King of kings.

So the change in family values that comes from a new first loyalty will inevitably challenge family relationships.

Changed family values: A new first longing

Finally, the genuine disciple of Jesus who understands the times will have a new first longing. Verse 39 requires careful thought if we are to understand it properly. On initial reading, the first half of the statement appears rather enigmatic and hard to pin down. What did Jesus mean when he said, *'whoever finds his life will lose it'*? The key to making sense of what Jesus was saying comes in the second half of the verse: *'whoever loses his life* for my sake *will find it.'* In other words the phrase *'finds his life'* is to be understood in terms of finding meaning and purpose in life without reference to Jesus. If a person finds meaning, purpose and direction to life without reference to Jesus, then no matter how 'worthy' their life is, they will ultimately lose it. Once again, it is at the cross that this truth becomes plain, for at the cross we see that God's judgment must fall on anything and anybody who lives with their own plans or their own status and ambition at the very heart of their life. The cross shows us that God must judge and punish sin. Sin is a matter of living my life without reference to God. Were it possible for sinners to be accepted in his kingdom without the just judgment of sin, we can be sure that God would have found some other way to call his people to himself. However, the fact that Jesus faced the just anger of his loving Father on the cross on our behalf gives us ample evidence that God's just anger is precisely what is waiting for those who insist on living for self without reference to Jesus. Those who seek to find their life apart from Jesus will lose their life eternally. Conversely, as a person finds meaning and purpose in Jesus, so they start to live for his sake. From the perspective of the world, such people will appear to lose their lives, for they will no longer live just to please themselves. However, Jesus' sin-bearing death and triumphant resurrection indicate that anyone who *'loses his life for my sake'* will ultimately be vindicated.

Such a change in family values will inevitably bring a change in family relations. The context of this whole section of Matthew's gospel involves the proclamation of the gospel. This means that those believers who understand the times will be proclaiming that *'the kingdom of heaven is at hand'* (chapter 10 verse 7). They will follow Jesus' command to *'say in the light'* what they have *'heard in the dark'* and will *'proclaim on the housetops'* what they have heard *'whispered'* (verse 27). Right at the heart of the new values of a disciple of Jesus will be the desire to make known the glorious kingdom of the King of kings. We saw the same thing with the two blind men in chapter 9, who *'went away and spread his fame through all that district'* (verse 31).

C T Studd was the famous nineteenth century equivalent of Ian Botham or Kevin Pietersen. Aged 21, he played at the Oval in Kennington in a test match which England appeared to be about to win but lost, finally, to the Australians by 8 runs in the closing minutes. It was as a result of that match that the term 'the Ashes' was coined. Apparently, play was so exciting in that in the closing hour one spectator chewed through the handle of his umbrella! In the 1880s, Studd made the decision to stop playing cricket and set sail to China to take the gospel to the Chinese. He understood the times. Before he left England, a series of meetings was held in Bermondsey, just ten minutes away from where I live in London. At one of these meetings, he said this:

> How could I spend the best years of my life in working for myself and for the honour and pleasures of this world while thousands and thousands of souls are perishing every day without having heard of the Lord Jesus Christ, going down to Christ-less, hopeless graves?[4]

C T Studd is just one famous example of a Christian disciple who understood the application of these verses. The changed values of a Christian disciple involve a new first love, a new first loyalty and a new first longing. It is not hard to see how such changed values will bring a change in family relations.

Before we leave these verses we need to notice that they do not apply simply to unusual or special Christians like C T Studd.

---

[4] *The Cambridge Seven* J C Pollock p. 71 published by IVP 1955

Five times in three verses (37-9) Jesus uses the word *'whoever'*:

> "Whoever loves father or mother more than me is not worthy of me … whoever loves son or daughter more than me is not worthy of me … whoever does not take his cross and follow me is not worthy of me … Whoever finds his life will lose it …whoever loses his life for my sake will find it."

Clearly, these words apply to every Christian, whatever their condition, profession or situation. They are not just for 'super-hero' Christians, they are for us all of us, and they come in a chapter whose content is full of the command to proclaim the gospel publicly.

The everyday Christian who does not love Jesus in his work more than any other tie or connection is not worthy of Jesus, says Jesus; the everyday Christian who does not hate their own personal sin and seek to put themselves and their agenda to death is not worthy of Jesus, says Jesus; the everyday Christian who does not consider their longing to be a farmer, a doctor, a dentist, a teacher, a mother, even, to be less important than their desire to be first and foremost a Christian, will end up losing their life eternally.

Do you see what Jesus is asking of us, as we understand the times in which we live? We are to be first and foremost a Christian, placing Jesus and his work and our love for him first. This means that whether you are a banker, a utility worker, a teacher, a taxi driver, a medic, a musician or a mother, you will see yourself first and foremost as a full-time gospel worker. As we make Jesus our first love, our first loyalty and our first longing, there will be consequences in the way we spend our time, the way we use our money and the way we set our goals and ambitions. Little things like our daily decisions; big things like how we raise our kids, or what we do with the 20 or 30 years of our 'retirement' that might be used in his service.

This makes it all the more important for us to be clear on the reason for the change in family values. We need to remember that our change in first love, our desire to put self to death, and our longing to gain life in God's new creation, all come as a result of grasping what happened on the cross.

At weddings, I sometimes ask the bridegroom to pause in the middle of the excitement of the day and ponder the cross. I suggest that he should take his eyes off his bride for a moment, forget the honeymoon and the holiday plans, his speech and the champagne, and that he should think instead about Jesus. Although Jesus was rich, yet for our sakes he became poor, so that we through his poverty might become rich; though Jesus was in very being God, he did not count equality with God a thing to be taken and exploited for his own end. Jesus made himself nothing, he emptied himself into the form of a slave, and being found in human form, he humbled himself and became obedient to death, even death on a cross (2 Corinthians 8 verse 9; Philippians 2 verses 6-8).

It is possible that a person can have been living as a Christian for many years and yet can have grown slightly discontent or disillusioned in their Christian life. It is even possible for someone facing the hard grind and daily challenge of full-time, paid Christian ministry to grow slightly disgruntled in their work. If that is the case, it will certainly be because they have lost sight of the cross of Jesus and all that it means. As we meditate on the cross, we will find that we cannot but love Jesus with all our heart, mind, soul and strength; we will find that our desire to put to death everything that Jesus hates will be re-kindled; and we will find that we will long to live out this changed value system wherever God has placed us, knowing that our decision to 'lose life' for his sake will be vindicated by him at the end of the age.

Conversely, just as these verses spell out for us the source of the change of values that will energise us to live differently, so they identify the very things that will keep us from 'losing our life'. The things that keep a person from losing life for Jesus' sake are love of family, loyalty to self, and a longing for the prizes of this world.

I spend a lot of time talking to young men and women as they are making career decisions that will affect the rest of their lives. In many cases their parents long for them to be successful in the eyes of the world. Some may have made enormous sacrifices in order for their children to be able to achieve the things they consider to be most important. Some parents move house in order to get their children into the right school, others will have sweated over their children's homework with them. For many, the underlying assumption has been that their children should get the best test results in order to get into the best school, so as to be able to get the best exam results in order to get into the best university, which in turn will enable them to achieve the best degree so as to get the best CV, so as to get the best career. All this so that the children in turn will have the best opportunity to maximize their potential in a life lived out with no reference to their creator. It is not surprising that friction follows when parents find out that their children do not share their own ambitions.

I remember speaking to the relatives of a young man who had just qualified as a surgeon. He was an extraordinarily capable young man and had graduated as one of the top students of a well-known London medical college. I was speaking to some distant relatives of his shortly after he had announced that he was going to start training for paid Christian work. The relatives were very upset by his decision, and eventually one of them exclaimed, 'it's such a waste'. These people claimed to be Christians, but in reality their longing for the prizes of this world was keeping them from godly joy at their family member's desire to 'lose his life'.

Whilst what Jesus has to say in chapter 10 concerns every Christian, it may be the case that as you have been reading these words, God has been speaking to you about the possibility of paid, full-time Christian ministry. It may be that you know that you have the gifts, that those gifts have been tested and proven in your local church, and that you have the track record of a godly man or woman about which Paul speaks in 1 Timothy 3 and Titus chapter 1. If that is the case, I wonder, do you understand the times? Jesus has laid out the terms and conditions of discipleship and he has explained the ties of his kingdom. Here are three things that might keep you from making the next move in your Christian service: first, a love of family above a love for Jesus; secondly, a loyalty to yourself instead of a loyalty to Jesus; thirdly, a longing for what this world has to offer rather than a longing for Jesus' agenda. As you spend time meditating on the cross of Jesus Christ, his glorious resurrection and his enthronement as Lord of heaven and earth, you should find these three things being put into their proper perspective and, as the children's chorus puts it, 'the things of earth will grow strangely dim in the light of his glory and grace'[5].

A change in family fortunes

Having laid out for us the change in family relations that comes from a change in family values, Jesus closes this discourse by speaking of the change in family fortunes. Once again it is significant that the reward is future, not present.

> "Whoever receives you receives me, and whoever receives me receives him who sent me. The one who receives a prophet because he is a prophet will receive a prophet's reward, and the one who receives a righteous person because he is a righteous person will receive a righteous person's reward. And whoever gives one of these little ones even a cup of cold water because he is a disciple, truly, I say to you, he will by no means lose his reward."

---

[5] Helen H Lemmell, *'O soul, are you weary and troubled?'*

The 'prophet' in these verses refers to the person who proclaims the truth about Jesus, the 'righteous person' is the person who has been made right with God, and the phrase 'little ones' in Matthew's gospel always refers to Jesus' disciples (Jesus makes this explicit here with the words *because he is my disciple*).

As we think about these verses, we need to realise what a big thing it would have been to receive somebody like this in a first century Palestinian village. In rural villages, even today, people know one another's business. To receive a prophet or a righteous person in the context of chapter 10 would be to receive somebody who had come into the village proclaiming publicly that Jesus is God's long-awaited King (see verses 7, 12-14 and 27). Were we to have received such a person and offered hospitality to them in our home, everybody in the village would have come to hear about it. Our reception of such a person, who was engaged in the activity of gospel proclamation, would have been a public declaration that we were associating openly with Jesus, his people and his message. So Jesus was speaking about those who line up publicly alongside those who stand publicly for him. As we do so, we will receive the rich reward of a prophet and a righteous person from our Father in heaven in his kingdom.

There was a girl in our church who came up to me after I had spoken on a passage such as this one. She was in her early 20s and was working for a television news broadcaster. Her boss was in his late 40s. She told me that since the day she had first made it public that she followed Jesus, her boss had made a point of regularly ridiculing her for her faith in front of all her colleagues. She wondered, was she doing the right thing? To my mind there was nothing wrong with her discipleship. Indeed, she was doing the very thing that Jesus was speaking about in these closing verses of the discourse. She was lining up publicly with those who stand publicly for the gospel of Jesus Christ. On account of her change in values, she was facing a change in her networks and connections – her boss was expressing his hatred of Jesus by directing his bullying sarcasm towards one of Jesus' disciples. This scene is repeated day after day across the world wherever we find any true disciples of Jesus. One day those who have stood openly and publicly with and for Jesus Christ will meet their Lord face to face. He will acknowledge them before their Father in heaven. Together, God the Father and God the Son will welcome them into the new creation, and as they are embraced by the only one who matters, they will hear those glorious words reserved for the prophet and the righteous and all who stand with them: 'well done, good and faithful servant.' (Matthew chapter 25 verse 21)

Isaac Watts provides the perfect words for any man or woman who understands the times in which we live:

> Forbid it, Lord, that I should boast,
> save in the death of Christ my God;
> all the vain things that charm me most -
> I sacrifice them to his blood.[6]

Suggested Questions for group or personal study

1. Why are Jesus' words in verses 24-26 so shocking?

2. Verses 37-39 show the reason why family members might turn against true disciples of Jesus. What are the three reasons given? To whom do these verses apply?

3. What does it mean to love Jesus more than father or mother? Why might a person do that?

4. What does it mean to take up one's cross and follow Jesus? Why might a person do that?

5. What does it mean to lose life for Jesus' sake? Why might a person do that?

---

[6] *When I survey the wondrous cross*

6. In verses 40-42 Jesus identifies incentives for realigning ourselves with his people. What are they?

7. Jesus is speaking in a context where everybody would have known one another's business. What would it have meant to 'receive a prophet' or to 'give one of these little ones a cup of cold water because he is a disciple'? What is the equivalent in your place of work and the place where you live?

8. Why would a person want to do these things?

9. In summary, what are the big lessons you have learned from Matthew chapter 8 to 10? How has your life changed as a result of studying these chapters?

Preacher's Note 1

It would be well worth looking closely at several commentaries on these verses and observing how the commentators treat them. Time and again there is little effort taken to see how they relate to one another. As preachers, it is not good enough for us to treat them as a string of independent, isolated and unrelated comments. Our task is prayerfully to seek the logic that holds this part of the discourse together. Once again, this will take much time in prayer, study and thought. I am convinced that the verses provide an explanation as to why discipleship is so divisive. You may not find my explanation adequate, but before you set out to preach on these verses, you will need to have been shown a more convincing alternative!

PARTNERSHIP

PHILIPPIANS WILLIAM TAYLOR

CONCISE, PORTABLE SPIRITUAL FOOD

Partnership
Concise, portable spiritual food - Philippians
William Taylor

The church at Philippi is considered to be one of the model churches of the New Testament.

But if this were a report at a shareholders' meeting we might be asking ourselves whether the Chairman has really got this right? Is something being hidden? It seems too good to be true! If this were an athlete we might be asking ourselves whether there has been some performance-enhancing substance in the diet! And if this were an end-of-term report we might be asking ourselves if the teacher had got the right child!

Can a church really be that good?

But there's no doubting that Paul has the right church. Perched on the edge of Southern Greece, Philippi was the first city to hear the Christian message in Europe - we have much to learn from the church that grew there.

This fresh and lively study book is ideally suited to the more interactive way we learn in today's church.

ISBN 9781845502317

TEACHING
AMOS

Unlocking the Prophecy of Amos
for the Bible Teacher

BOB FYALL

SERIES EDITORS: DAVID JACKMAN & ROBIN SYDSERFF

TEACHING
ACTS

Unlocking the book of Acts
for the Bible Teacher

DAVID COOK

SERIES EDITORS: DAVID JACKMAN & ROBIN SYDSERFF

SPIRIT OF TRUTH

Unlocking the Bible's Teaching on the Holy Spirit

DAVID JACKMAN

TEACHING
1 PETER

Unlocking the book of 1 Peter
for the Bible Teacher

ANGUS MACLEAY

SERIES EDITORS: DAVID JACKMAN & ROBIN SYDSERFF

Other books from PT Media:

Teaching Acts:
Unlocking the book of Acts for the Bible Teacher
David Cook
ISBN 978-1-84550-255-3

Teaching Amos:
Unlocking the prophecy of Amos for the Bible Teacher
Bob Fyall
ISBN 978-1-84550-142-6

Teaching 1 Peter:
Unlocking the book of I Peter for the Bible Teacher
Angus MacLeay
ISBN 978-1-84550-347-5

Teaching Matthew:
Unlocking the Gospel of Matthew for the Expositor
David Jackman
ISBN 978-1-85792-877-8

Spirit of Truth:
Unlocking the Bible's Teaching on the Holy Spirit
David Jackman
ISBN 978-1-84550-057-3

TEACHING
JOHN

Unlocking the Gospel of John
for the Bible Teacher

DICK LUCAS & WILLIAM PHILIP

SERIES EDITORS: DAVID JACKMAN & ROBIN SYDSERFF

TEACHING
THE CHRISTIAN HOPE

Unlocking Biblical Eschatology
for the Bible Teacher

DAVID JACKMAN

SERIES EDITORS: DAVID JACKMAN & ROBIN SYDSERFF

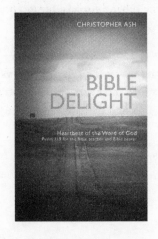

CHRISTOPHER ASH

BIBLE
DELIGHT

Heartbeat of the Word of God
Psalm 119 for the Bible teacher and Bible hearer

Teaching John:
Unlocking the Gospel of John for the Bible Teacher
Dick Lucas & William Philip
ISBN 978-1-85792-790-0

Bible Delight:
Psalm 119 for the Bible Teacher and Bible hearer
Christopher Ash
ISBN 978-1-84550-360-4

Teaching the Christian Hope:
Unlocking Biblical Eschatology for the Expositor
David Jackman
ISBN 978-1-85792-518-0

Preaching the Living Word:
Addresses from the Evangelical Ministry Assembly
edited by David Jackman
ISBN 978-1-85792-312-4

Christian Focus Publications

publishes books for all ages

Our mission statement –

STAYING FAITHFUL

In dependence upon God we seek to help make His infallible Word, the Bible, relevant. Our aim is to ensure that the Lord Jesus Christ is presented as the only hope to obtain forgiveness of sin, live a useful life and look forward to heaven with Him.

REACHING OUT

Christ's last command requires us to reach out to our world with His gospel. We seek to help fulfil that by publishing books that point people towards Jesus and help them develop a Christ-like maturity. We aim to equip all levels of readers for life, work, ministry and mission.

Books in our adult range are published in three imprints.

Christian Focus contains popular works including biographies, commentaries, basic doctrine and Christian living. Our children's books are also published in this imprint.

Mentor focuses on books written at a level suitable for Bible College and seminary students, pastors, and other serious readers. The imprint includes commentaries, doctrinal studies, examination of current issues and church history.

Christian Heritage contains classic writings from the past.

Christian Focus Publications, Ltd
Geanies House, Fearn,
Ross-shire, IV20 1TW, Scotland, United Kingdom
info@christianfocus.com